# 24 BY 24

## THE 24 HOUR PLAYS ANTHOLOGY

EDITED BY

MARK ARMSTRONG AND SARAH BISMAN

**Playscripts, Inc.**

Published by Playscripts, Inc.
450 Seventh Avenue, Suite 809
New York, New York, 10123
www.playscripts.com

Cover design by Shine Advertising Co., LLC
Text design and layout by Jason Pizzarello

First Edition: April 2009
10 9 8 7 6 5 4 3 2 1

ISBN-13: 978-0-9709046-9-0

Library of Congress Cataloging-in-Publication Data

24 by 24 : the 24 Hour plays anthology / edited by Mark Armstrong and Sarah Bisman. -- 1st ed.
    p. cm.
  ISBN 978-0-9709046-9-0 (pbk.)
  1. American drama--21st century. I. Armstrong, Mark, 1972- II. Bisman, Sarah. III. Title: Twenty-four by twenty-four.
  PS634.2.A12 2009
  812'.608--dc22
                                    2009002665

# Contents

# Foreword

As an actor, I can only describe appearing in The 24 Hour Plays as the purest adrenaline rush you can imagine. The experience is magical, moving, frightening and heart-stopping. And, as Artistic Director of The Old Vic Theatre in London, I have had frequent cause to bless the talented guys who thought of this ultimate theatrical challenge.

The 24 Hour Plays were brought to me by Old Vic producer Kate Pakenham in 2004, after she had seen them in New York, and have remained at the heart of what the Old Vic does ever since. That year we ran the first of our annual Celebrity galas with many well-known, much-loved actors, including Jim Broadbent and Brian Cox, to raise important money for our education, community and emerging talent programme. It seemed the perfect project to throw open to young talent and, in 2005, The 24 Hour Plays: Old Vic New Voices for 18-25 year old actors, writers, directors and producers was born.

Over the years we've worked with Tina Fallon and The 24 Hour Company on the programme in the UK, we have all seen the transforming effect of The 24 Hour Plays process on young practitioners. Over 150 artists have taken part and all report an incredible feeling of achievement, a building of confidence, and a real growth and development of their skills as collaborators and artists. The creative relationships forged during this process are deep, fruitful and long-lasting, with over 150 productions and readings coming life as a result of peer networking. The company of young actors, writers, directors and producers are chosen from thousands of applications, with hopefuls applying from across the country. We look for individuals not only with extraordinary creative flair, but those who understand and are enthused by the benefits of collaborative working. There can be no prima donnas in our line-up. Each successful applicant becomes a member of our New Voices Club (in a mentoring programme that lasts 3 years), and everyone who gets to the audition stage of the selection process becomes an associate member. We now have 5,000 young practitioners who have been touched by the 24 Hour experience. In 2007, we brought our mission to inspire and support emerging talent to New York, forming the New Voices Network—an exact counterpart of the New Voices Club in London—with its own first 50-strong company. The 24 Hour Plays came back to their American roots.

Every time I see The 24 Hour Plays, I marvel at the process. Regardless of whether each play was performed in a garage or on a Broadway Stage, or at The Old Vic, each is the culmination of just one day's work. With peer practitioners who only met the day before. In an unfamiliar theatre. With just minutes of tech time. No dress rehearsal. No prompt book. No safety net. The experience is magical. And I think it reminds you why you fell in love with theatre in the first place.

—*Kevin Spacey*
*London*

# Introduction

The first production of The 24 Hour Plays was supposed to be our last. In 1995, inspired by Scott McCloud's 24 Hour Comics, a motley band of theater artists, musicians, novelists and friends gathered to produce an evening of short plays. In one day. And then perform them. For a live audience.

Honestly, we didn't know if it would work. We had legal pads, typewriters, a cantankerous photocopier and a Polaroid camera. I remember looking out at the assembled team and thinking, Oh shit. We actually have to do this. And, remarkably, we did.

Thirteen years later, we are no longer surprised that The 24 Hour Plays process works. But it still feels like a miracle every time. Hundreds of playwrights and directors, and over a thousand actors have participated. Along the way the event has raised money for good causes and produced plays that have gone on to greater rewards—as well as some of the noblest failures ever to reach the stage.

The process is simple. Six writers, six directors and two dozen actors gather at ten o'clock the night before the show. Everyone brings a prop and a costume. Each participant is photographed and writes a One-Line Bio. The rules are announced, the schedule rehashed, and then everyone introduces his/her prop, costume, and self. Actors give a brief description of their skills (sing? dance? accents?), and tell the group what they would love to do onstage (speak German? die? play an accordion?). Writers take notes. The production staff keeps it all humming along. It's like the first week of summer camp played at fast-forward. Strangers meet, expose their innermost secrets, bond, and then go off to sleep for the night.

Except, of course, the writers. No sleep for them! They select casts, like choosing an intramural volleyball team. (Some writers are particularly canny at casting. David Lindsay-Abaire is a great example; Elizabeth Berkley, Andrew McCarthy, Rachel Dratch, Cheyenne Jackson, and Cady Huffman—who knew?) Around midnight, the writers finally settle down to their laptops with coffee and snacks, their heads crammed with props, costumes, and skills, the hopeful faces of their casts staring up from the Polaroids. No pressure...

By 6:00 am, the plays are complete. A flurry of photocopying ensues, and an influx of fresh production staff keeps the ball rolling. Directors appear, grimly, at 7:00 am. Each reads every play, not knowing who wrote what. It's a good thing the writers are gone, as even the funniest scripts elicit no laughs. The room is silent, thick with concentration. The directors submit their choices, cross their fingers and hope for the best, certain that the other directors' lists are identical to their own. Not so, however: the choices are always eclectic, and most directors get their first or second picks.

Actors arrive at 8:30 am, eat breakfast, and receive their scripts. Rehearsals begin at 9:00 am, and continue until the extremely brief tech rehearsals start at 5:00 pm. Throughout the day, designers and stage managers try to foresee every possibly technical need. As that is impossible, tech rehearsals are as fraught as, well, tech rehearsals. With only 20 minutes to run a cue-to-cue, directors are tense and tempers can flare—especially if the previous show ran over for any reason. "Director X got a half-hour! Why do I only get fifteen minutes!?!" is a common refrain. Whatever, people. Deal with it. We have a show in two hours. Tech may be bitchy, but it's brief. The tight schedule ensures that most of the plays have never been performed off-book, in full dress, with lights and sound, until there is an audience present.

Why does it work? Is it because the audience understands that they are witnessing a heroic effort? Because the performers are so fused to one another by the intensity of their experience? Or because, in a spirit of unqualified collaboration, every person is permitted to do work that is at once brave and humble?

Or maybe people just love a good stunt.

Whatever the reasons, the engine of The 24 Hour Plays has kept us very busy. From 1995-1999, Crux Productions oversaw the event. A "boutique" (read: underfinanced) production management company, Crux juggled clients like Primary Stages and The Atlantic Theater Company while producing its own small theater projects. When the economics of that arrangement proved unwieldy, we formed The 24 Hour Company in 2000. We took our ethos from the new economy: a virtual office, with no overhead, and a single, laser-like focus—to produce The 24 Hour Plays. Armed with that philosophy, the new company—now consisting of me, Lindsay Bowen, Kurt Gardner, Philip Naudé, Sarah Bisman, and Lou Moreno—managed the growth of the Plays. Strategic partnerships with The Culture Project, Planet Impact, Working Playground, Urban Arts Partnership, The Old Vic (London), Soulpepper (Toronto), The Kennedy Center American College Theatre Festival, The William Inge Theatre Festival, The Exchange and others helped The 24 Hour Plays grow into an international force without ever maintaining a static office, mailing address, or even a telephone number.

Over the years we have tried some variations on our central theme. Some succeeded brilliantly, like the Cold Readings series and The 24 Hour Musicals. Some mercifully bit the dust, including a couple of failed television pilots, The 24 Hour Films, and an attempt at podcasting. Turns out theater people are particularly skilled at, uh, making theater.

In September 2001, we produced our first "celebrity" benefit. Financed by credit cards and arriving just three weeks after the attacks of September 11th, the event was a watershed moment for the Plays and the wider theatrical community. Some of the finest actors in New York—Phillip Seymour Hoffman, Julianne Moore, Billy Crudup, Liev Schreiber, Lili Taylor, Sam Rockwell, Rosie Perez, Mary-Louise Parker, Andre Royo—joined the cast. A young actress named Scarlett Johansson skipped school to perform. Warren Leight made us laugh again, Christopher Shinn made us cry, and a new annual event was born.

Throughout our history, The 24 Hour Company has been able to maintain the good will of the New York theater community by adhering to a few basic rules of conduct: always respect the space and staff of your host theater, leave the place cleaner than you found it, be liberal with meal penalties, get it in writing, and the golden rule—good fences make good neighbors. The Atlantic, The Vineyard, Signature Theatre Company, 45 Bleecker Theater, Teatro La Tea, the Theatorium, The Lucille Lortel, the Minetta Lane, PS 122, The Ohio Theatre, The Orchard Project, The American Airlines Theater, Joe's Pub, and BAM have all hosted The 24 Hour Plays. We are grateful to them and their dedicated crews for putting up with our insane schedule and unexpected technical needs. Although I don't believe the Local One stagehands really minded giving Elizabeth Berkley a (fully-clothed) shower…

We are lucky to have a new generation of theater artists to help us keep moving ahead. With the Old Vic in London, we have created The 24 Hour Plays: Old Vic New Voices as an incubator for fresh talent. Our high school and college licensing programs introduce the process to young people, some of whom have never considered theater as a viable, non-geeky form of expression. Here in New York, At Play Productions (a group assembled through the first Stateside version of The 24 Hour Plays: Old Vic New Voices) will produce the Off Broadway season of The 24 Hour Plays. We are in good hands, and we look forward to the next chapter.

In the meantime we have this volume to remind us that it's not all smoke and mirrors. Sometimes, in spite of ourselves, great art gets made. These plays, be they light and comedic or somber and sublime, are evidence that contemporary playwrights will give you more than you bargained for—if you simply ask for the impossible.

—*Tina Fallon*

Catherine Tate and Wallace Shawn
in *Toccata and Fugue*

The 24 Hour Plays on Broadway
The American Airlines Theatre, 2006
Photo: Katvan Studio

# Editors' Note

This book and the years of amazing work it represents would not have been possible without the vision and dedication of Tina Fallon, who is one of the great unsung heroes of the American theater. Sarah Bisman, Lindsay Bowen, Kurt Gardner, Lou Moreno and Phillip Naudé are also some of the finest people I've ever had the pleasure to be associated with. I'm deeply grateful to the whole 24 team. For Playscripts, Jason Pizzarello and Kimberly Lew worked tirelessly to make this book happen.

*—Mark Armstrong*

The 24 Hour Company is aided in all of our efforts by a dedicated group of designers, programmers and volunteers, who we thank immensely. Thanks to our graphic design team at Shine for yet another brilliant piece of work. I have been extraordinarily lucky to have two terrific mentors during my time in New York City: Warren Leight and Tina Fallon. My relationship with The 24 Hour Company exists because of them, and I thank them for all of their support. Love and thanks to my family and friends, and to The 24 Hour Company (truly my second home). My profoundest gratitude is reserved for Mark Armstrong, who is a terrific co-editor, friend, and fierce champion of The 24 Hour Plays. We have been dreaming of an anthology for years, and without all the efforts of Mark, Jason Pizzarello, and Playscripts, we'd still be imagining "what if?"

*—Sarah Bisman*

The cast and crew of *Jack on Film.*

Back row: Sarah Tuft, Ryan Mekenian
Middle row: Sam Rockwell, John Hawkes, Erika Christensen
Front row: Matthew Lillard, Ian Morgan

The 24 Hour Plays on Broadway
The American Airlines Theatre, 2006
Photo: Katvan Studios

The cast and crew of *The Blizzard*.

Back row: Aasif Mandvi, Bennett Miller
Front row: Fisher Stevens, Anna Paquin, Gaby Hoffman, David Ives

The 24 Hour Plays on Broadway
The American Airlines Theatre, 2006
Photo: Katvan Studios

# SLEEPING CITY
## by John Belluso

# BIOGRAPHY

John Belluso's plays include: *The Poor Itch* (produced by The Public Theatre), *A Nervous Smile* (produced by the Actors Theatre of Louisville's Humana Festival of New Plays), *The Body of Bourne* (produced by the Mark Taper Forum), *Henry Flamethrowa* (produced by Trinity Repertory Company, Victory Gardens Theatre and Studio Dante), *The Rules of Charity* (produced by the Magic Theatre), *Body Songs*, created with legendary theatre director Joseph Chaikin (Eugene O'Neill Center/NPC, workshopped at the NYSF/Public Theater), *Traveling Skin*, and *Gretty Good Time* (produced by the Ensemble Studio Theatre, Perishable Theatre, Falcon Theatre, and by VSA arts at the John F. Kennedy Center for the Performing Arts). Awards and Honors include a National Endowment for the Arts/Theatre Communications Group Playwright-in-Residence Grant for a residency at the Atlantic Theatre in New York, the AT&T On-Stage Award, the Mark Taper Forum's Sherwood Award, the VSA arts Playwright Discovery Award as well as grants from the New York Foundation for the Arts, the Berrilla Kerr Foundation Award and honorable mention for the Kesselring Prize. In addition, from 1999 to 2002, he served as Co-Director and from 2002-2005 as Director of the Mark Taper Forum's Other Voices Project for Disabled Theatre Artists—one of the nation's only professional developmental labs for theatre artists with disabilities. Mr. Belluso received his Bachelors and Masters degrees from NYU's Tisch School of the Arts Dramatic Writing Program where he studied with Tony Kushner, John Guare, Tina Howe, and Eve Ensler, among others.

## ACKNOWLEDGMENTS

*Sleeping City* was originally produced as a part of The 24 Hour Plays Benefit for The New York State September 11 Victims Relief Fund on February 24, 2002 at the Henry Fonda Theater in Los Angeles. It was directed by Gregory Mosher and featured the following cast:

PROFESSOR BRINE .............................................. Jared Harris
BEN .............................................................. Seth Green
LOIS / DORIS ......................................................Gina Phillips
OTTO .....................................................................Adam Nelson

## CAST OF CHARACTERS

PROFESSOR BRINE
BEN
LOIS
OTTO

# SLEEPING CITY

*A street corner in New York City,* BEN *is in a wheelchair, he wheels in to where* PROFESSOR BRINE *is standing, leaning up against a building.* BRINE *is rubbing his glasses, trying to clean off a spot, he spits on the lens.*

**PROF. BRINE.** *(Speaking to* BEN*:)* That's disgusting right? Spitting on my glasses. I'm trying to get rid of the streaks and spots. Sorry if that was disgusting.

**BEN.** Well, uh, it's okay, you need to uh, you, I'm sure you needed to clean your glasses, my girlfriend does that same exact thing, with her glasses, oh yes.

**PROF. BRINE.** Yes. Yes. And now, I do believe, that they are clean. I have excreted much saliva to serve this purpose and the results are looking good!

*(*BEN *looks around as if he is looking for someone or something.)*

**BEN.** Usually there's so many people on the streets, but there's no one here.

**PROF. BRINE.** It's 3 AM.

**BEN.** Yes, but even so, New York City.

**PROF. BRINE.** Do you, need something?

**BEN.** *(Pointing:)* There's a hill. I came down here to the deli, I needed some milk. I really needed some milk. But there's a hill to get back up there, between 118th Street and 119th there is a pretty steep hill, up to my dorm, my dorm room, the building, it's up there on 119th Street. It was easy coming down the hill of course, just, coasted right down, kind of fun actually, breezing right down! Uh, but I could really use a push, if you wouldn't mind, to get back up the hill.

*(A pause.)*

**PROF. BRINE.** Yes. I'll give you a push.

*(Pause.)*

Yes, I never noticed there was a hill there before. Yes. Of course. Let's go.

**BEN.** My name's Ben. Benjamin. Ben.

*(*LOIS *and* OTTO *walking through the streets of lower Manhattan.)*

**LOIS.** I have so many things inside of me! It's ridiculous how much I have; I have muscle fibers and spit and piss and love; a whole heart full of love is what I have and he doesn't know how to deal with any of it!

**OTTO.** He shouldn't be allowed to be cruel to you.

**LOIS.** I take care of him, like he was my baby and not my boyfriend and I don't want a fucking baby I want a man. I want to feel super. I think I deserve to feel super.

5

**OTTO.** You're a pretty lady and you've got a good fat brain with lots of thoughts and ideas in it, and that's a good think to have, most women don't have brains like yours.

**LOIS.** *(Smiling at him:)* Thank you, Otto. Thank you. *(Suddenly reticent:)* I don't know if we should go down there. What is there to see, It's just a huge crater now, a hole in the ground. Why do people want to go down and see it? I want to go down and see it.

**OTTO.** Me too. Are we on a date?

**LOIS.** What?

**OTTO.** We had dinner, and we were laughing together before, I told you several jokes and they all made you laugh, and now we're walking through the streets together. Is this a date?

**LOIS.** I already have a boyfriend.

**OTTO.** You hate him.

**LOIS.** *(Smiles, sighs, a dreamy look in her eyes:)* Yeah.

    *(*PROF. BRINE *is struggling, pushing Ben's wheelchair up the hill.)*

**PROF. BRINE.** Oh God, you're heavy!

**BEN.** No, I'm not! The higher you go up the hill the harder it gets, it's physics at work.

**PROF. BRINE.** No, it's ME at work and I'm going to get a bloody hernia. Although I will say; my buttocks muscles are getting quite a workout. *(Pauses, feeling his buttock muscles.)* I can feel my buttocks muscles getting quite firm indeed.

**BEN.** Oh, well, that's good.

**PROF. BRINE.** *(Pushing on:)* Yes, it is. So you live in the dorms, a student at Columbia?

**BEN.** Freshman. I couldn't sleep. Kept having nightmares. Terrible nightmares. About the Trade Center. Being in a wheelchair and being trapped in there. And I'd wake up. The only thing that helps me get back to sleep is if I eat about three bowls of cereal and milk, so I really needed some milk.

**PROF. BRINE.** I see.

**BEN.** You're a professor at Columbia, I've see you around the campus.

**PROF. BRINE.** Literature, American Poetic Tradition, my specialty. If you ever find yourself in my class you will be doused with so much Walt Whitman they'll be plucking Leaves of Grass out of your anus.

**BEN.** That, is disgusting. And by the way; you smell like whiskey and body odor.

**PROF. BRINE.** Well, yes, I've had a few sips of whiskey tonight, a few hundred sips of whiskey, and I'm a bit nervous, so I suppose I may be perspiring.

**BEN.** Why are you nervous? What, are you out roaming the streets at three in the morning trying to scope out a prostitute?

**PROF. BRINE.** Oh, really! The thought of it!

*(They both crack up laughing, laughing loud, the laughter dies down.)*

**PROF. BRINE.** Prostitutes, yes exactly. Indeed. But I've been looking around from corner to corner and I just can't seem to locate any. Have you seen any?

**BEN.** No, I… *(Looking across the street, discreetly pointing:)* Her, uh, there, on the other side of the street…

**PROF. BRINE.** Oh, her… Do you think she's a…

**BEN.** Not sure, she's all dressed up, but she might just be walking home from a fancy party or something. *(Shocked, looking closer:)* Oh, Oh, well it looks like she's, she seems to be…

**PROF. BRINE.** She's lifting up her skirt and showing us her kitten.

**BEN.** Her "kitten"?

**PROF. BRINE.** Yes, her kitten, that's what I call it.

**BEN.** *(Looking back at her:)* Oh. Her kitten.

*(LOIS and OTTO walking further downtown.)*

**LOIS.** Canal Street. It's not to late for us to turn back.

**OTTO.** I thought you wanted to see it.

**LOIS.** I do want to see it, I'm afraid. People are traveling from all over the world to see it, they built a special viewing platform.

**OTTO.** So it's okay.

**LOIS.** I don't know, maybe it's, like healing, a healing thing to be able to see it, to see the site. Morbid curiosity maybe. It's a mass grave, it really is, oh god, why are we going to a mass grave?

**OTTO.** This definitely isn't a date, not a date, I can see this very clearly now. This is not a place where people go on dates.

**LOIS.** I told you, I have a boyfriend, I love him, we've been together for years, he gives me problems. But you and I, we're only going to be friends, Otto. That's all there will be between us.

**OTTO.** He's, he's…

**LOIS.** He's what?

**OTTO.** You said, he's in a wheelchair?

**LOIS.** Yes. He is.

**OTTO.** Why? What happened to him?

**LOIS.** High School Prom, really, really drunk. Southern Comfort mixed with cherry coke. He hit an oak tree. Car split right in half.

**OTTO.** And you, you stayed with him, you stayed his girlfriend, even then?

**LOIS.** Yes, I took care of him. I still do. Now we both study at Columbia, together. *(Very softly:)* I care for him like a baby, I listen to his nightmares, I bring him cereal and milk to help him sleep, but I don't need a baby, I need a man.

**OTTO.** I, am a man.

**LOIS.** You, are a Burger King worker. You gave me a free whopper with cheese and asked me to take a walk with you when your shift ended.

**OTTO.** And you said "yes." *(Moving in very close to her, his lips close to her, teasing:)* You said "yes." Didn't you?

> *(He kisses her, she gently resists at first, then reciprocates. They're kissing grows passionate.)*
>
> *(*PROF. BRINE *pushing the wheelchair.)*

**PROF. BRINE.** *(Grunting, struggling as he continues to push the wheelchair up the hill:)* This, is getting, quite difficult, yes indeed.

**BEN.** Did you want to go back down there to the young woman who revealed her, uh, private area to us? If you'd like, I could just try and push myself up the rest of the hill and you could go back there and, accompany her…

**PROF. BRINE.** Don't be silly. Besides, she wasn't what I fancy. Her feet were too small.

**BEN.** Oh, you like women with big feet?

**PROF. BRINE.** Enormous feet. Oh, God! The bigger the better. Fat and long and round and bulbous! You realize, under normal circumstances I wouldn't admit this fact to a stranger, particularly not to a student, but whiskey gives me wings.

> *(Pause.)*

And I hate my life. It's easy to be open with embarrassing desires when you hate your life.

**BEN.** Yeah. My girlfriend, she smothers me. She wants to take care of me, be like a nurse to me. And I hate that, I fucking hate it. I'm not broken, I'm a student at Columbia University, I'm not broken, I'm doing fine. Plus I hate her glasses. She wears these old lady glasses, they make her look ugly, buttfucking ugly. I fucking hate those fucking glasses!!!

> *(*LOIS *and* OTTO *standing, she puts on her glasses.)*

**LOIS.** Do you like my glasses?

**OTTO.** Oh yeah, they're very retro. But the good kind of retro, the kind that is anticipating what the next retro trend will be, and they don't take themselves too seriously, which is important for glasses. *(Pointing:)* There it is.

> *(Bright lights shine on them.)*
>
> *(Her eyes widen, her hands start to shake.)*
>
> *(Tears coming to her eyes.)*

**LOIS.** *(Softly:)* Ground Zero. *(A little louder:)* I want to go home. Okay? Take me home.

**OTTO.** Calm down, it's just…

**LOIS.** Don't fucking touch me. *(Losing control:)* I want to see Ben, my cripple boy Ben, I want to see my love.

*(OTTO holds her tight.)*

**OTTO.** Okay yeah, okay, I'll take you to Ben, to see your love. Yeah.

*(PROF. BRINE, pushing struggling, over-the-top grunts and groan sounds; they are finally reaching the top of the hill.)*

**PROF. BRINE.** We made it, we're at the top of the hill. *(Pointing:)* Is that your dorm?

**BEN.** Yes. But I don't want to go in yet. I just want to sit here, and look at the city. The lights, slowly lighting up, one by one, coming awake, after nightmare sleep.

**PROF. BRINE.** *(Gently placing his hand on* BEN's *face:)* The nightmares will end.

**BEN.** No. They won't.

**PROF. BRINE.** "In midnight sleep, of many a face of anguish
Of the look at first of the mortally wounded—of that indescribable look;
Of the dead on their backs, with arms extended wide,
I dream, I dream, I dream."

### *End of Play*

# THREE GUYS AND A BRENDA
## by Adam Bock

# BIOGRAPHY

Adam Bock's *The Thugs* premiered at NYC's Soho Rep in 2006, winning an OBIE for playwriting for Mr. Bock and an OBIE for directing for Anne Kauffman, and was named to both of TimeOut NY's Top Ten lists. His new play *The Receptionist* received its world-premiere at Manhattan Theatre Club in October 2007, directed by Joe Mantello. His play *The Drunken City* received its premiere at Playwrights Horizons in early 2008.

*Five Flights* played Off-Broadway at Rattlestick Theater in 2004, after a five-month sold-out run at San Francisco's Encore Theater in 2002. The play won the Glickman Award, and was nominated for the American Theater Critics Award, the Elizabeth Osborn Award, and two BATCC Awards. It has been published in *Breaking Ground*, an anthology of new plays edited by Kent Nicholson.

Shotgun Players' production of *Swimming in the Shallows* won the 2000 Bay Area Theater Critics Circle Awards for Best Original Script, Best Production, and Best Ensemble. *Swimming in the Shallows* was a Clauder Competition Award-winner, an L. Arnold Weissberger Award nominee, an LA Weekly nominee, a GLAAD Media Award nominee, named to TimeOut NY's Top Ten, and has been produced in Los Angeles, London, San Francisco, Boston, Providence, Santa Cruz, Ithaca, Key West, Long Beach, Toronto, Montreal, and the Edinburgh Fringe Festival, as well as Second Stage's Uptown Series in New York City in the summer of 2005.

Mr. Bock helped Jack Cummings III develop *The Audience*, nominated for three 2005 Drama Desk Awards including Best Musical. His play *The Shaker Chair*, produced by Actors Theatre of Louisville in the Humana Festival in 2005, was nominated for the Kesselring Prize. *The Typographer's Dream* has been produced in New York City and San Francisco, and at the Edinburgh Fringe Festival, and in Berkeley in 2006. Mr. Bock's play *Thursday* was produced in San Francisco with a 2003 NEA grant.

These and other plays have been read or workshopped at New York Theater Workshop, Playwrights Horizons, NYC's Vineyard Theater, Soho Rep, Underwood Theater, Rude Mechanicals NYC, the JAW/West Festival at Portland Center Stage, Printer's Devil, Oregon Shakespeare Festival, Magic Theater, Salt Lake Actors Company, Southwark Theater, TheatreWorks' New Works Festival, New Works at Perry-Mansfield, and Clubbed Thumb. Mr. Bock is an artistic associate at Shotgun Players and Encore Theater, and is a resident playwright at New Dramatists.

## ACKNOWLEDGMENTS

*Three Guys and a Brenda* was originally produced by The 24 Hour Company at The Atlantic Theater in New York City on March 15, 2004. It was directed by Garret Savage with the following cast:

BOB.................................................................Julie Shavers
JOE.................................................................Carla Rzeszewski
RANDALL.....................................................Jama Williamson
BRENDA.........................................................Tami Dixon

*Three Guys and a Brenda* won the Heideman Award and received its world premiere at Actors Theatre of Louisville's 30th Anniversary Humana Festival of New American Plays on April 1st and 2nd of 2006. Made possible by a generous grant from The Humana Festival, and presented by special arrangement with William Morris Agency, LLC. This play was directed by Steven Rahe with the following cast and staff:

JOE.................................................. Suzanna Hay
BOB.................................................Keira Keeley
RANDALL.................................... Cheryl Lynn Bowers
BRENDA........................................ Sarah Augusta
Scenic Designer..........................................Paul Owen
Costume Designers............................... John P. White
                                                                       Stacy Squires
Lighting Designer.................................... Paul Werner
Sound Designer................................Benjamin Marcum
Properties Designer............................. Mark Walston
Stage Manager.................................Debra Anne Gasper
Assistant Stage Manager...................... Heather Fields
Assistant Stage Manager................Paul Mills Holmes
Dramaturg...................................... Julie Felise Dubiner

All production groups performing this play are required to include the following credits on the title page of every program:

> *Three Guys and a Brenda* received its World Premiere in the 2006 Humana Festival of New American Plays at the Actors Theatre of Louisville.

## CAST OF CHARACTERS

BOB, a man, played by a woman
JOE, a man, played by a woman
RANDALL, a man, played by a woman
BRENDA, a woman, played by a woman

## SETTING

At work.

# THREE GUYS AND A BRENDA

*Before this,* BOB, JOE *and* RANDALL *were watching TV waiting for their shift to start.*

*Now:* BOB *and* JOE *are onstage. They are crying.*

RANDALL *walks across stage, crying. Exits.*

BOB *and* JOE *continue to cry.*

RANDALL *walks onstage. He is still crying. He has a roll of toilet tissue. He hands out tissue. They are all crying.*

BRENDA *walks across stage. They try not to/don't cry when she is onstage. She exits.*

*They cry again. Deep breaths.*

*They sniff. They sniff. They sniff.*

BRENDA *enters.*

**BRENDA.** You guys are on second shift right?

**JOE.** Yeah Brenda.

**BOB.** Yeah that's right.

**BRENDA.** Joe, then when your shift starts, then you and Bob are going to show Randall what to do with the new machine, ok?

**JOE.** Ok.

**BRENDA.** Ok?

**BOB.** Yeah ok.

**JOE.** Ok sure.

**BRENDA.** Ok then.

    *(Exits.)*

**JOE.** *(Deep breath, doesn't cry:)* Fucking animal nature shows.

**BOB.** I know.

**JOE.** They get me every time.

**RANDALL.** She's so beautiful.

**JOE.** She is.

**BOB.** She is Randall.

**JOE.** Yes she is.

**RANDALL.** Isn't she Bob? She's beautiful!

**BOB.** She is Randall.

**RANDALL.** I have to tell her she's beautiful.

**BOB.** I don't know Randall.

15

**JOE.** I don't know.
**BOB.** What do you think Joe?
**JOE.** I don't know about that Bob.
**BOB.** Yeah me neither I don't know either.
**JOE.** Might not be appropriate. In the work environment.
**BOB.** Right.
**JOE.** Right?
**BOB.** In the work environment.
**JOE.** This being work.
**BOB.** Right.
**RANDALL.** I have to.
**BOB.** Well if you have to, you have to.
**JOE.** That's right.
**BOB.** If you have to, you have to.
**JOE.** Right.
**BOB.** Right.
**JOE.** But I don't think you're going to.
**BOB.** Nope.
**JOE.** Right?
**BOB.** Nope!
**RANDALL.** I have to.
**BOB.** Joe here might.
**JOE.** That's something I might tell her.
**BOB.** Right. Joe might.
**JOE.** I might. I might say something to her like
**BOB.** Like
**JOE.** "You're beautiful!"
**BOB.** Right!
**JOE.** But I don't know whether you'd say something like that.
**RANDALL.** I am too. I am too going to say something like that to her!
**JOE.** Well.
**BOB.** Well.
**JOE.** Well ok then.
**RANDALL.** Because I think she's beautiful.
**BOB.** Well.
**JOE.** Ok then.
**RANDALL.** And I'm going to say it.

**BOB.** Ok then.

**JOE.** Ok.

    *(*RANDALL *exits.)*

**JOE.** Think he's going to tell her?

**BOB.** Nope.

**JOE.** I'm not watching any more of those nature shows. They're too sad.

**BOB.** Yeah I know. Me neither.

**JOE.** They're too fucking sad. They make me sad.

**RANDALL.** *(To audience:)* Thing that's hard about being a guy? You always have to tell the girl "Hey you're great" or "Hey I think you're great" or "You're great" or "You're great" and "Would you maybe want to go out?" and that's hard. Plus it's hard to have to shave all the time. That's hard too.

**JOE.** *(To audience:)* Plus it's hard to pick a good deodorant.

**RANDALL.** *(To audience:)* Yeah that's hard too.

**JOE.** *(To audience:)* Plus guys? Plus we have to carry everything.

**RANDALL.** *(To audience:)* Right.

**JOE.** *(To audience:)* Especially heavy things. Like sofas.

**RANDALL.** *(To audience:)* Yeah that's hard.

**BOB.** *(To audience:)* Plus

**JOE.** *(To audience:)* Plus you have to drive all the time.

**RANDALL.** *(To audience:)* Yeah. And that.

**BOB.** *(To audience:)* Plus

**JOE.** *(To audience:)* You have to drive on really long trips, to the beach, to visit your family, and then back from the beach. And if a tire blows you have to take it off, you have to put the spare on. Plus you have to pay.

**RANDALL.** *(To audience:)* For everything.

**BOB.** *(To audience:)* Plus

**JOE.** *(To audience:)* Plus sometimes you don't understand something and that can make you feel stupid and so you have to pretend you understand it. That can be hard. *(Pause.)*

**BOB.** Yeah.

**RANDALL.** Yeah. *(Pause.)*

**JOE.** *(To audience:)* That can be hard. *(Pause.)*

**RANDALL.** *(To audience:)* Mostly it's hard though saying "I think you're great" and "Would you maybe like to go out" and then you have to wait and find out what the answer is. That's hard.

    *(*BRENDA *enters.)*

**RANDALL.** Um. Brenda?

**BRENDA.** Give me a second.

*(BRENDA exits.)*
**RANDALL.** Guys. Don't bust my chops.
**JOE.** I didn't say anything.
**RANDALL.** Don't bust my chops.
*(BRENDA enters.)*
**RANDALL.** Hey Brenda?
**BRENDA.** I said just give me a.
*(She exits.* JOE, BOB, *and* RANDALL *stand.)*
*(RANDALL looks at* JOE *and* BOB.*)*
*(BRENDA enters.)*
**BRENDA.** Yeah ok?
**RANDALL.** Oh yeah so. Um.
**BRENDA.** Yeah?
**RANDALL.** Guys?
**JOE.** Oh yeah.
**BOB.** What?
**JOE.** Ok. Come on.
**BOB.** What?
**JOE.** Bob come on.
**BOB.** Oh yeah yeah ok!
**JOE.** Ok!
**BOB.** Ok.
*(They exit.)*
**RANDALL.** Yeah so Brenda?
**BRENDA.** Yeah ok?
**RANDALL.** So.
**BRENDA.** I have work Randall.
**RANDALL.** Um.
**BRENDA.** Yeah ok so, what?
**RANDALL.** Um.
**BRENDA.** I have work.
*(Turns to exit.)*
**RANDALL.** I think you're beautiful.
**BRENDA.** What?
**RANDALL.** Um.
**BRENDA.** That's not funny.
**RANDALL.** What?

**BRENDA.** That's not funny.

**RANDALL.** I'm not being funny.

**BRENDA.** That's mean. That pisses me off. That really truly pisses me off.

**RANDALL.** No I do.

**BRENDA.** I have a lot of work. And you're pissing me off.

**RANDALL.** No I do. I think you're beautiful. I think you're beautiful like a. Like something beautiful. Like the sun in the sky. Like a lake. Like the sunshine on a lake in the early evening right before the sun goes down and everything is calm. And the water's calm. That's what I think.

**BRENDA.** Shut up.

**RANDALL.** No I do.

**BRENDA.** Like a lake?

**RANDALL.** Like the sunshine. On the lake.

**BRENDA.** Really?

**RANDALL.** Yeah really.

**BRENDA.** Really?

**RANDALL.** And I think If only I could kiss her I'd be happy.

**BRENDA.** Really?

**RANDALL.** Yeah.

**BRENDA.** You think if you kissed me, you'd be happy?

**RANDALL.** Yeah.

**BRENDA.** You want to kiss me?

**RANDALL.** Yeah.

**BRENDA.** And that would make you happy?

**RANDALL.** Yeah.

**BRENDA.** Just a kiss?

**RANDALL.** Yeah.

**BRENDA.** Ok so.

**RANDALL.** Really?

**BRENDA.** So?

*(They kiss. Should be a good smooch.)*

**RANDALL.** *(Softly:)* Yeah. That made me happy.

**BRENDA.** I have work.

**RANDALL.** Ok.

**BRENDA.** I have work.

**RANDALL.** Ok. Ok.

*(She exits.)*

**JOE.** *(To audience:)* I told my wife I loved the sound of her voice on the phone. And I do. I still do.

**BOB.** *(To audience:)* I gave my girlfriend a smooth stone I found on the side of the road.

**JOE.** Right?

**BOB.** Yeah.

> (RANDALL *smiles.*)
> *(The three men sit.)*

## *End of Play*

# ANOTHER BEAUTIFUL STORY
## by John Clancy

## BIOGRAPHY

John Clancy is an OBIE award winning director and Executive Artistic Director of Clancy Productions, Inc. He is the founding Artistic Director of Present Company and a founding Artistic Director of The New York International Fringe Festival. He is an award-winning playwright and his productions have toured the world. He has been honored with five Scotsman Fringe Firsts at The Edinburgh Festival Fringe, two Best of the Festivals at the Adelaide Fringe Festival, a Glasgow Herald Angel Award for direction and a New York Magazine Award for "creativity, enterprise and vision." In 2007, his company was awarded the inaugural Edinburgh Festival Award by the Edinburgh International Festival and commissioned to create a new work for the Festival. He serves as the Executive Director of the League of Independent Theater, the advocacy organization for 99-seat theaters and their practitioners in New York City. He lives on the Lower East Side with his wife and partner, Nancy Walsh.

## ACKNOWLEDGMENTS

*Another Beautiful Story* was originally produced by CRUX (The 24 Hour Company) at The Present Company Theatorium in New York City on September 5, 1998. It was directed by Oleg Kheyfets with the following cast:

NARRATOR ........................................................... Henry Tenney
LEAD .................................................................... Valerie Stanford
ARTY GUY ........................................................ Christian Martin
FOURTH CHARACTER ........................... Jonathan Butterick

## CAST OF CHARACTERS

NARRATOR, old school, classically trained, beautifully voiced actor, working for the audience in that old trouper way.

LEAD, young, charming, every bit as old school, but has that desperate slightly wide-eyed audition energy of someone who should be getting gigs but for some reason isn't and it's starting to get to her, goddamn it.

ARTY GUY, straight to it, low-key, no performer energy at all. Doesn't see lead as a legitimate threat or challenge. This is his living room.

FOURTH CHARACTER, sweet, simple, just doing what he or she was told to do. No opinion, no problems, no acting.

# ANOTHER BEAUTIFUL STORY

NARRATOR *enters from upstage center, uniform, top hat, cane, dead sunflower. Walks slowly to center stage, maintaining kindly but direct eye contact with audience. Waits a beat and begins.*

**NARRATOR.** The Narrator stands center stage. The narration begins. Not with his words, but before he speaks, before he pauses, upon his entrance, the narration begins. It's an old story he has to tell you, one you know, one you nod to, one you whisper to each other at night. An old but wonderful story. And I, as your Narrator, your humble but firm voice of reason, would like to take this moment before all the hullabaloo begins and the stage becomes peopled with strange yet familiar visages, before the magic begins to mist the gulf between you and I, I your Narrator, your friend and trusted guide, would beg to extend my thanks and gratitude to you, for listening. Again. For coming and listening to me. You are gathered. We are met. The stage is lit, the audience attentive and without any warning whatsoever, the Narrator suddenly drops dead.

*(He does so. Drops. Straight. No big death scene. Way long pause, a second longer than seems necessary.* LEAD ACTRESS *pokes her head out from behind curtains stage left. Looks at* NARRATOR. *Smiles at audience. Goes back behind curtain. Speaks to someone. Pokes head back. Smiles. Walks over to* NARRATOR. *Kicks him. No response. Smiles at audience.)*

**LEAD.** Um. I'm playing the lead in this um…piece. There's a story that should be sort of…laid out for you so that my ah, character makes sense and so that you can, you know…enjoy it, but um… *(Kicks* NARRATOR *again.)* Well. I could tell you the story. Or the part that refers to me anyway. I didn't really study the rest of it so much, you know, 24 hours to learn all your lines, less actually, we got the scripts this morning and I'm in another piece as well which makes a lot more sense, actually, sort of a clearer narrative than this one, but I know the basic, ah, outline of this one, so I'll be the Narrator and then I'll do the Part and then you know. That's what we'll have to do. So, um, the story is—

**ARTY GUY.** *(From audience:)* Excuse me, miss.

**LEAD.** Yes?

**ARTY GUY.** I'm sorry to interrupt here.

**LEAD.** No please, I could use the help.

**ARTY GUY.** But I mean, haven't we seen this before? I mean, all of this, right down to me being out in the audience, pretending to disrupt? Narrator dies, actor drops character, self-examination of the act of theater blah blah blah? I mean, it's 1998. Haven't we done this, haven't we seen this? I know

23

you didn't write this you're probably a fine, serious artist, but we've been here before. My god. Is there nowhere else to go?

**FOURTH CHARACTER.** *(Appears Upstage Right, groovy green jacket, Hamburger Helper, red polka dot ball.)* I'm the fourth character. Apparently at some point late last night the writers were told they had to have a minimum of four characters so that all the actors would get parts. Thus, I was conceived very late and only in the spirit of obligation and pretty much after the play was thought through, so there is no character here really. I'm a coat rack for this costume pretty much. I'm a vehicle for these props. That's as deep as I get. Sorry to interrupt.

**ARTY GUY.** Again. The self-examination, the self-reflexive view of the writing process, Barthes did this years ago and better, this whole po-mo shell-game of identity and character, of act and purpose, the arbitrary nature of signified and signifier, words and objects being linked, I mean, this is undergraduate shit here, excuse me, but come on.

**LEAD.** Most of my experience has been in more traditional and musical theater so I don't know about the po-mo things you're talking about, but would you like to come onstage because I'm completely upstaging you here and I can't really adjust.

**FOURTH CHARACTER.** I'll be right back *(Disappears behind curtain).*

**ARTY GUY.** Yeah, I'll come onstage, I mean, I'm an actor, that's where I belong. *(Gains stage.)* Here now, that's a little better. Two of us, onstage, traditional, characters, audience, dead guy.

**LEAD.** Do you want to do the play?

**ARTY GUY.** We're doing the play, we're two and a half minutes into the play, a quarter of the way through.

**LEAD.** No, I mean the story.

**ARTY GUY.** The Narrator died. Get it? Voice of Authority, Reason, Cause and Effect, Calming, Old School Master Storyteller comes out, dies, leave us to Flail about and Create Meaning on our Own? Yes? Have you read a book in the last forty years? Seen the news?

**FOURTH CHARACTER.** *(Enters wearing a Hawaiian shirt and carrying a huge sewing needle.)* Hey. Different costume. Huge sewing needle. Still no real character.

**ARTY GUY.** And this guy? The Man Without Qualities. Right?

**LEAD.** Boy I'm really hating this.

**ARTY GUY.** *(To FOURTH CHARACTER:)* Come out here.

**FOURTH CHARACTER.** Can I get another prop?

**ARTY GUY.** Forget about the prop. Just come here.

**FOURTH CHARACTER.** I don't have any more lines.

**ARTY GUY.** Forget about the lines. Come here.

*(*FOURTH CHARACTER *joins them center stage.)*

**LEAD.** *(To* FOURTH CHARACTER:*)* Do you want to do the play?

**FOURTH CHARACTER.** I don't have any more lines.

**ARTY GUY.** So here we are. Arty-smarty guy from the Audience, Lead musical comedy girl and guy with no Lines but a Big, what the fuck is that, a sewing needle? A Big sewing needle. And the Dead Narrator. This is it folks. This is what we fucking got right here.

**LEAD.** *(Desperate to save the day and summoning all her training and good will:)* But all is not lost, friends, for there is a story to tell here.

**ARTY GUY.** There is no story, the Narrator is—

**LEAD.** We will tell the story ourselves, my friends.

**FOURTH CHARACTER.** I don't have any more lines.

**LEAD.** Let's try, come on, let's try to remember.

**ARTY GUY.** The story is there is no story, that's the point here, No storyteller, no one listening—

**LEAD.** They're here. They're listening. We're here. We can—

**ARTY GUY.** Who are they to listen to us? What do we have to say to them? Who gives us the right to speak?

> *(The following lines are simultaneous, each character taking it right to the audience, not competing, just communicating simultaneously, until* LEAD *silences all.)*

**LEAD.** *(Best storytelling energy, really trying, don't fake it:)* Once upon a time there was a beautiful, beautiful princess and she lived in a land where it was always beautiful and warm and beautiful and she lived there very happily with all of her beautiful things and she was very happy and everything was beautiful. Until one day an ugly man came out of the audience, came out of the forest where all the ugly, nasty animals lived and where it was dark and terrifying and not beautiful and he came into the palace, into the sacred, beautiful palace where the princess lived and he said, no, no, pomo, blah blah, and he killed the King! He killed the King! The King died and the Princess said shut up shut up and tell the story just shut up shut up SHUT UP.

**ARTY GUY.** *(Very calm, simple, direct:)* Come on folks. Here we are way in the hell east of everything downtown, I mean, where are we? This isn't even the East Village, we're below the East Village, it's Labor Day weekend, obviously we're a theater crowd, we've read all the books and what are we doing? Yes, I know, this was written in one night, the words I'm speaking now were scribbled in pencil on an oversize legal pad right upstairs at 1:46 in the morning and then typed up at 3:12, the writer had been up all day, all night and now well into the morning, so we're not expecting genius, but we should at least, here, now, expect originality, something fresh, but what is there to say? Honestly. What is there to do? Now? Here?

**FOURTH CHARACTER.** *(Apologetically, would like to help, but…)* I don't have any more lines. I don't have any more lines. I don't have any more lines. I don't have any more lines. I don't have any more lines. I don't have any more lines. I don't have any more lines. I don't have any more lines etc.

**LEAD.** *(Furious. But in that scary, controlled, pissed off way:)* We are going to tell a story. All of us. To these people. Here. Now.

**ARTY GUY.** *(Exhausted, to a child:)* The Narrator is Dead.

**LEAD.** All right. Perfect. Do you know what happens when you stop believing? Somewhere, a Narrator dies. When little girls and boys and downtown theater types stop believing in Stories and Structure and Beginning Middle and End, and a Simple Goddamned Text goddamn it, a narrator dies. Do you believe? Do you believe in stories? If you believe, if you really believe, clap your hands. Clap your hands if you believe. Clap. Clap your hands if you believe.

*(*FOURTH *claps, half-heartedly, trying to help out, embarrassed.)*

Thank you! Thank you! Clap harder! Everyone clap. Clap. Clap! CLAP! CLAP!

*(Stick with it until audience claps. Believe.)*

Yes! We believe. We believe!

*(*NARRATOR *lies dead.* LEAD *kicks him.)*

Get up. Get up. They believe. At least they're playing along. Get up!

*(*NARRATOR *twitches, wakens, begins to struggle to his feet.)*

Yes! Yes! We believe! O thank you, thank you children, thank you boys and girls, Thank You!

*(The instant* NARRATOR *gets to his feet fully, all other characters drop dead. Instantly. No fuss. Straight to the ground.)*

**NARRATOR.** And so my friends, a magical tale. Of life and death and rejuvenation and the power of belief. Of princesses and ogres and mad fools without much to say, but with so much to, ah, carry. And so, as the page turns and you close the book of this evening, remember me, your humble, ever faithful narrator. It is not the storyteller, but the story that remains, but without the storyteller there is no story to tell and the story is eternal, the story is all, the story is *(*NARRATOR *puts his hand to his heart worriedly.)* Shit. *(He drops dead. Other characters spring to life.)*

**ARTY GUY.** See? Us or him. Don't go bringing him back to life. If he's dead, let him stay there.

**FOURTH CHARACTER.** I'm going to get another prop. *(Exits.)*

**LEAD.** I just don't get this stuff. I never have. I try, but, I don't know. I don't get it.

**ARTY GUY.** You were great. Are you kidding? You did a great job.

**LEAD.** No, I just, you know, I mean, thank you, that's nice, thank you but you know, what's the point? What are we doing?

**ARTY GUY.** Hey, we did it. It's over. That's it. That's the piece.

**LEAD.** Well great. That was great. Can we bow or would that be counter-revolutionary or whatever?

**ARTY GUY.** Bow, baby. Get the prop boy out here.

**LEAD.** We're taking our bows! Come on out here!

(FOURTH CHARACTER *enters with as many large and odd props as possible, a wig and anything else backstage, joins them.*)

**ARTY GUY.** Come on dead guy, big bow.

(NARRATOR *rises. They join hands and bow to some big showy, upbeat music. They bow too much, too enthusiastically. They kiss each other, applaud each other, give each other flowers if possible. Almost weeping with the joy of having given such a precious gift to the audience, they slip gracefully back behind the curtain.*)

## *End of Play*

# RAY SLAPE IS DEAD
## by Mike Doughty

## BIOGRAPHY

Mike Doughty is a singer/songwriter. He lives in Brooklyn.

## ACKNOWLEDGMENTS

*Ray Slape Is Dead* was originally produced by The 24 Hour Company at The Atlantic Theater on the set of *An Adult Evening of Shel Silverstein* in New York City on October 21, 2001, with the following cast:

RED BANK HANK .................................................... Andy Slade
RAY SLAPE ...................................................... Jonathan Rossetti
DEXTER JUNIOUS ................................................ Paul Urcioli
HARRIS FRANTZ.................................................... Joe Latimore

## CAST OF CHARACTERS

RED BANK HANK
RAY SLAPE
DEXTER JUNIOUS
HARRIS FRANTZ

# Ray Slape Is Dead

**HANK.** What do you call a musician without a girlfriend?

**RAY.** Homeless.

**HANK.** How many guitar players does it take to change a light bulb?

**RAY.** Twenty Seven.

**HANK.** One to change the light bulb, twenty six to stand around and say, hey, man, I could do that. What do you call a trombone player with a beeper?

**RAY.** An optimist. How do you know there's a girl singer at the door?

**HANK.** She can't find the key, and she doesn't know when to come in.

**DEXTER.** Ray Slape is dead. As I'm telling you this, I mean, as of now, Ray Slape is dead. But we're backtracking. OK. So back a few years, and Ray Slape loves this girl named Betty. And Betty is really fine, she's delicate and sweet, but she's young, and Ray Slape is young, and neither of them know what's going on. So the school year ends, and young wide-eyed Ray Slape goes to the beach with ample-bootied Betty and her two roommates, who are equally foxy. And in the cab ample-bootied Betty turns to Ray Slape and tells him she doesn't love him and it's over. And so Ray Slape goes:

**RAY.** I don't think I should go to Jamaica with you.

**DEXTER.** And ample-bootied Betty says, oh but Ray, Ray let's be friends, why can't we be friends? Why can't we just go to the beach as friends? Ray Slape is the guy who can't displease anybody. So ample-bootied Betty breaks Ray's heart and then drags him on this nightmare vacation.

**RAY.** The weed was REALLY good.

**DEXTER.** And Ray is just completely wasted, you know? In this verdant setting, with the salt water, the floral smell. It's so erotic, the air is charged, and Ray's grief is just massive. They're all sharing a cabin, Ray Slape and the three foxy girls, and Ray and ample-bootied Betty are sharing a bed.

**RAY.** I was REALLY high.

**DEXTER.** And every time he shifts towards ample-bootied Betty, every time he just brushed up against her, she moves away. Like it's horrifying to her.

**RAY.** But I really can understand where she's coming from.

**DEXTER.** And they're in this skeezy tourist town where all these Jamaican hustler guys are always prowling around, trying to entice these extremely stoned tourists into giving them money. And they keep seeing Ray walking around, looking forlorn, with these three foxy girls, and they call out, Hey man!

**RAY.** Sad clown, turn that frown upside down!

**DEXTER.** You've got three! Give me ONE!

**HANK.** That is freaking funny man.

**DEXTER.** Anyway Ray's got to come back home before everybody else. Because Ray and Red Bank Hank and me have this band. And we've got a show to do.

**HANK.** Fucking yeah!

**DEXTER.** And Ray decides he's going to smuggle a little weed home.

**HANK.** Fucking let's do it!

**DEXTER.** So he puts it in his shoe. And as it turns out, he comes like yay close to being busted—this whole nightmare situation of narcs and dogs. But he doesn't get busted. And he gets back home, and he tells me this story—

**RAY.** I almost got busted. I'm shaking, look at me, what do I do now?

**DEXTER.** And so I tell him—what you do now is get me and Hank high immediately.

**RAY.** I want to be in a band with a girl singer.

**HANK.** What are you, like, super nutty, my man? The way you sing? Those songs? They're beautiful, my friend, I mean they're just like—fucking yeah. Right on. I mean really, right on.

**DEXTER.** They were really beautiful. The way he sang was really, really beautiful.

**HANK.** You don't need a—man, a girl singer? Man—naw! Naw, man. What are you, like—uh uh. I mean fucking yeah!

**DEXTER.** But I was thinking, like always I'm thinking, and I'm thinking— Hank is a drummer. And in every band—

**HANK.** I mean—pfft!—fucking yeah!

**DEXTER.** —there must be a drummer. But Ray has something. This beautiful thing that's just him, really. And I don't have it. But what's wrong with me? Why should I not be special? What's unspecial about me? Ray?

**RAY.** I really think we should find a girl singer.

**DEXTER.** If you stick with me and Hank—

**HANK.** Yeah!

**DEXTER.** I think you're going to be fine. Because—don't knock yourself. You've got a little something. You know, it's not a lot but it's something, and me and Hank—we AMPLIFY it. We take what you've got, Ray, and we make it bigger.

**HARRIS FRANTZ.** I'm an old Warner Brothers guy. If you cut me, I bleed Bugs Bunny!

**DEXTER.** Things slowly got better for our little band.

**HARRIS FRANTZ.** I can tell just looking at you that you are EX-TREMELY serious young men, EXTREMELY serious young men. I'm telling you, as I stand here, you will get outrageous phones on this song. Outrageous!

**DEXTER.** And of course this manager guy that picked us up is totally blowing smoke up our ass.

**HARRIS FRANTZ.** You know—here's the thing about hit records—it's all about the songs. Which one of you writes the songs?

**RAY.** I write the songs.

**DEXTER.** We all write the songs.

**RAY.** I write the song part of the songs?

**DEXTER.** We write all the songs together. Isn't that right Hank?

**HANK.** Fucking yeah! All for one bay-bee!

**DEXTER.** And really the fact was that all the money was in who wrote the songs. And why should Ray get all the money? Look.

**HANK.** Fucking them is some dope fuckin' songs you got Ray, man.

**DEXTER.** That we've got.

**HANK.** Fucking yeah!

**DEXTER.** So we made a record, and we're out on the road. And, you know, the truth is, we're sniffing a lot of dope.

**RAY.** I met this beautiful girl the last time we played Stockholm.

**DEXTER.** She was a porker, Ray. And, you know, she really didn't want to fuck you Ray. She wanted to fuck me.

**HANK.** I fucked NINE GIRLS in Stockholm!

**DEXTER.** This one night Ray gets on stage, and he's pretty high, and he stumbles up to the mic and he goes—

**RAY.** I wrote this song about a girl named Betty, who I loved so much—I mean, I really loved her—and she didn't love me, and what are you gonna do? What are you gonna do?

**DEXTER.** And he's going on about ample-bootied Betty, and it was just pathetic, and I hated hearing it. So we get offstage, and I went to Ray and I said: Ray.

**RAY.** yeah?

**DEXTER.** Ray, you don't ever say that onstage again, okay?

**RAY.** But—

**DEXTER.** Look Ray. You think you're special, but actually—actually. I'm in this band too. I'm right here with you Ray. And that kind of bullshit just cuts me out of the deal.

**RAY.** Now look, you are just fucked. You are fucked! Why would you say that to me? How could you say that? You are fucked!

**DEXTER.** Oh yeah? Well who do you think you are, Ray? Just who do you think you are?

**RAY.** *(Looks shaken.)*

**DEXTER.** And that's how I won the argument. Because what I meant was—don't be so high and mighty. But what he heard was—who do you think you are. Who do you think you are.

**RAY.** I don't know who I think I am.

**DEXTER.** And he didn't say anything about writing the songs again. Ever again. And all the songwriting money, we split it even-steven.

**HARRIS FRANTZ.** Fellas. This is not a climate that takes real kindly to your kind of music. You know what they want? They want girl singers. Because they see you Ray Slape, and maybe they like the song, but the thing is, they don't want to BE you. They want to BE the girl singer. And as I have told you so many times, the marketplace is driven not by songs, but by the kids and who the kids want to be.

**DEXTER.** We were sniffing a lot of dope. We were schmeckers, real schmeckers.

**HARRIS FRANTZ.** We're gonna keep touring. We're gonna play to the base. That's what we're going to do until radio changes around a little. These huge records keep coming along, and they roll right over us. But we're going to keep playing to the base.

**DEXTER.** Ray started getting this asthma. Which of course was all about the dope sniffing, but Ray at this point, he was well into the dope, you know, we all were, but Ray, he's really fucked up with this dope-induced asthma. He starts like walking around like an old man. I mean, as in, little pitter-patter steps, if he exerts himself too much he has this life-threatening asthma attack. As in, he's crossing the street and he misses the don't walk sign.

**HANK.** Ray, man, you know, I'm thinking, this illness and everything? Maybe? It's like—maybe it's got something to do with the $300 you spend on heroin everyday?

**DEXTER.** One thing about Ray Slape is that when he had an idea he would leap out of his seat and start pacing in this really manic way. The guy was way clowny.

**HARRIS FRANTZ.** This thing you do, with the sad singing, and the hey-hey-hey, you know, that kind of, your version of who puts the RAM in the RAMALAMADINGDONG—heh heh heh—who puts the ram in the ramalamadingdong? You know. They're not buying that shit.

**DEXTER.** So one day Ray Slape gets this great idea, and he leaps out of his seat, and he has an asthma attack, and he's asphyxiating, and he dies.

*(*RAY SLAPE *leaves the stage.)*

**DEXTER.** And a lot of time goes by.

**HANK.** You know this kid I've got, he's freaking hilarious, man. Because, like, all he's into is waffles. That's it. His whole life is waffles. My wife's sister calls, and the kid gets on the phone and he goes—can you please come over and bring me some waffles? I mean, the mental landscape of this kid is waffles waffles and waffles. Always like this: can you make me some waffles?

**HARRIS FRANTZ.** So I have told you from the very first day that the music business, the world of music, it's like a circle. It's like a circle and it just keeps circling. Round and around. Do you follow me? OK. So things change. That's fact A. OK. Now first the kids, they liked the music, the Ray Slape kind of music—with the sadness and they hey-hey-hey, and then it was the girl singers who were all mad about all the things. And then it was the girl singers who were funny. And then it was the boy singers that were mad about the things, and then it was all the black guys with the shooting and the money. And now—I am telling you this just as I stand here—I swear to sweet sweaty baby Jesus on the unfilled grave of my beloved mother—

**HANK.** Can I have some waffles? Heh heh. Can I have some waffles?

**HARRIS FRANTZ.** Absolutely everything out there is sounding like Ray Slape. Every hit is like Ray Slape revisited.

**DEXTER.** And so the checks came flying in.

**HANK.** All fuckin' RIGHT!! I've got some waffles for you, buddy!! Heh heh.

**DEXTER.** And I was still sniffing the dope.

**HARRIS FRANTZ.** The poor kid with his problems and his demons, which you know he did not die in vain, for his beautiful art is moving millions. And now you and me got millions to move huh? HA HA HA HA…no, I don't mean to be crass, of course. But you know we all are extremely fortunate.

**DEXTER.** The thing is that when I asked Ray Slape who he thought he was, immediately I was cut in on the deal. And it was just an ego thing at the time, but then suddenly, years after his death, it was a gold mine. And then eventually things changed again.

**HARRIS FRANTZ.** This Ray Slape music is yesterday's news.

**HANK.** Waffles.

*(HARRIS FRANTZ and HANK exit the stage.)*

**DEXTER.** And the money started to run low. But I kept with the dope because I was pretty incapable of feelings and who knows what would happen if I stopped the dope and started feeling stuff again? And then one day I'm with that fat girl Felice at my apartment, and I owe her some bucks, but we're cool for the moment, and she leans down and does a bump, and then I do, and it kind of catches in my nose, and so I scratch it, and I look up, and there's fat Felice with a gun. And I say— Aw, naw, Felice. And the next thing I know I'm with fat Felice in my apartment, and I lean over and do a bump, and I look up, and there's fat Felice with a gun, and I say, Aw, naw Felice. And then I lean down and do a bump of dope, and I look up—and suddenly I'm noticing stuff around me. There's other people coming in and out of the apartment, and it's like they don't even see me. And across the street there's a guy and he's jumping off a roof. And then when he falls, suddenly he's back up, and he jumps again. And so I do a bump, and fat Felice has a gun, and I say, aw, naw Felice. And there's this guy and he's like choking there, and this other guy and it's like he's falling asleep. And then Ray Slape says:

**RAY.** We need to go.

**DEXTER.** But I think, no, Ray Slape is dead. And so I lean down and do a bump, and then I look up, and Ray says—

**RAY.** We need to go. You need to come with me.

**DEXTER.** And then suddenly I realize that fat Felice isn't there, and I can see all these people. Like everywhere there's a person who's dying in a different way—and Ray says we need to go.

**RAY.** It's time to go.

**DEXTER.** But I don't want to go. I really don't want to go, I couldn't tell you why but I just don't.

**RAY.** We need to go. It's time to go.

**DEXTER.** And so I guess that's when I let go, and we just went. You know? I don't know where it was we were going, but we just went. We just went.

### *End of Play*

# VAUDEVILLE, POPULATION TWO
## by Will Eno

# BIOGRAPHY

Will Eno's plays have been produced by the Gate Theatre, the SOHO Theatre, BBC Radio, the Rude Mechanicals Theater Company, and Naked Angels. He is a Helen Merrill Playwriting Fellow, a Guggenheim Fellow, and an Edward F. Albee Foundation Fellow. His play *The Flu Season* was recently awarded the Oppenheimer Award. His new play *Thom Pain (based on nothing)* premiered in August 2004 at the Edinburgh Festival (Fringe First Award, Herald Angel Award). It was produced in New York by Bob Boyett and Daryl Roth at the DR2 Theatre, and was named a Finalist for the 2005 Pulitzer Prize in Drama. Mr. Eno has recently been awarded the Alfred Hodder Fellowship, which includes a term at Princeton for the 2005-2006 academic year. His plays are published by Oberon Books, TCG, Playscripts, Inc., and have also appeared in *Harper's, The Antioch Review, The Quarterly,* and *Best Ten-Minute Plays for Two Actors*. He is presently at work on a new play, as well as a new translation of Ibsen's *Peer Gynt*. Mr. Eno lives in Brooklyn, New York.

## ACKNOWLEDGMENTS

*Vaudeville, Population Two* was originally produced by The 24 Hour Company at the Ohio Theatre in New York City on December 16, 2001. It was directed by Julie Bleha with the following cast:

ONE................................................................Veronica Newton
TWO .................................................................. Emily Helming

## DRAMATIS PERSONAE

ONE

TWO

## SETTING

Stage as currently set.

## STAGE PROPERTIES

Little pumpkin, guitar case, sombrero, snow machine.

# VAUDEVILLE, POPULATION TWO

ONE *and* TWO *enter.* ONE *holds little pumpkin, and wears a sombrero.* TWO *hold empty guitar case. Lights up.*

**ONE.** *(Comes downstage, strikes a pose, as if delivering a soliloquy:)* Nothing but limits, paltriness, vaudeville, crooked television, a broken snow machine—ridiculous trappings all for me to gently and without meaning die amidst.

*(*ONE *and* TWO *move snappily toward each other, stand too close together.)*

**TWO.** So guess what?

**ONE.** What?

**TWO.** I don't know.

**ONE.** You're kidding! That's great!

**TWO.** Thanks.

**ONE.** No, really. To be so honest. Just straight out: "I don't know." That's great.

**TWO.** Thank you. Really, seriously—thanks. But what about you?

**ONE.** I'm pregnant. And I have cancer. Of the uterus, of all places.

**TWO.** Wow. Cancer of the uterus. That's pretty serious.

**ONE.** I know.

**TWO.** They got you coming and going, didn't they?

**ONE.** I know. They did. I try to keep a sense of humor.

**TWO.** How so?

**ONE.** With jokes, and joking. I make them up out of the blue. For instance. So, let's see, this pregnant woman who's dying of uterine cancer walks into a bar. Just for a drink, you know, to kill some of the pain she feels all the time, both physical and emotional. The bartender goes, "Hey, why the long face?" And she goes, "I'm pregnant and I'm dying of uterine cancer, which, incidentally, has spread like crazy through me everywhere. By the way, the father left me." And everyone in there, everyone in the bar, goes, "I can't believe life would do something like that." And the woman goes, "It would. It really would. It did. It will again." Then the phone rings and the bartender is, like, "Hello?" But there's no one there. *(She laughs.* TWO *laughs.)* You have to laugh. Which is why I just laughed.

**TWO.** It's good we can laugh. Just what the doctor ordered.

**ONE.** Actually, the doctor ordered that my mid-section be blasted with a potentially lethal does of radiation until all my fingernails fall out and even the word "food" makes me violently sick to my stomach.

**TWO.** Yes, sirree. Good old laughter. Just what the doctor ordered. Oh, guess who I ran into?

39

**ONE.** Why, I don't know. Whoever did you run into?

**TWO.** Somebody named—I'm going to say—Michael? Miguel? Again, you know—I don't really know.

**ONE.** How mysterious. And so what did he say?

**TWO.** Honestly? Do you really want to know? Nothing.

**ONE.** Ah, life. Wonders seriously never cease. Can you believe, the young Mexican who impregnated me and gave me this sombrero was name Miguel. Ah, life. I go through each day as if in the night in my sleep someone drew glasses and a mustache on my face with a Magic Marker. I bear my sacred chalice down the aisle, toilet paper on my shoe, a sign that says "Destroy me," taped to my back.

**TWO.** Right. You know, you have to keep in mind that—wait, wait, hold on *(Begins to remove a hair from her mouth.)*, I've got a hair in my mouth. There. Ta-da! Look at that. How do you think that ever got in there? The craziest things happen to me. You're right. Wonders never cease. Seriously, they never cease. Do you know what I love about stuff like this?

**ONE.** Stuff like what?

**TWO.** I don't know. You know, stuff like this. *(Pause.)* Hey, my leg's asleep.

**ONE.** I'm going to die. We're going to die. Unhappily, in pain.

**TWO.** Did you even hear what I just said? *(Shakes her leg.)* Wake up, leg. There she goes. Now I feel it.

**ONE.** Yes, "Wake up, leg." Well said. My Mexican hat is off to you. Bravo. Muchas gracias. *(Pause.)* Ah, desperation. Ah, terrible friends. First-year Spanish. Tawdry tawdry life. The dismal theatre of appearances. The abysmal inner non-workings of the diseased and self-defeating self. All to end in a ridiculous trickle of artificial snow.

**TWO.** Do you like what I'm wearing?

**ONE.** Maybe you could play a song? *(Motioning toward guitar case:)* So I could cry. About my life. About which I have little or no feeling left.

**TWO.** Oh. This. *(Referring to guitar case:)* This is empty. It's sort of a metaphor.

**ONE.** Of course it is. *(Pause.)* I'm sorry, a question. Why, may I ask—

**TWO.** *(Interrupting, to finish the question:)* —do I carry it around if it's empty?

**ONE.** —do you think we're alive?

**TWO.** I thought you were going to ask a totally different question.

**ONE.** Forget it. You're right. Not important. No es muy importante.

**TWO.** No, I could try. "Why are we alive?" Hmm, hmm, hmm. It's a gooder, a real doozie. "Why are we alive?" You don't hear that one much anymore. *(Pause.)* You know, I really don't know. Huh. Isn't that funny? That

I wouldn't know something like that? Here I am all snappy and smug, all grown up and educated, and I don't even know, wouldn't even guess.

**ONE.** No es muy importante. *(Pause.)* Miguel said to me, "Carve a tiny little face in this pumpkin, for we do not have your pumpkin in Mexico."

**TWO.** Right, right.

**ONE.** Life goes on. The parade of feelings. I'll try to carve a little face in there.

**TWO.** Right, right. Listen, I'm going to leave off with you here. See you later. *(Pause. She moves downstage. To the audience:)* Well, we've had—I hope—a little fun here tonight. What you should, above all else, know, though, is that, in life, in your life—

**ONE.** *(Grabbing her stomach, she collapses in pain, with a scream.)*

**TWO.** *(To audience:)* I guess there's more.

**ONE.** *(She is dying.)* Miguel! Mi dios! *(It starts snowing.)*

**TWO.** Hey, it's snowing. It's a miracle. "Una milagro." Is that right, "milagro?"

*(Turning to* ONE:*)* Please don't die, Virginia—it's snowing.

**ONE.** My name isn't Virginia. This is killing me. My body is killing me. I didn't do anything to deserve anything like this.

**TWO.** It's close, though, right? Veronica, Valerie, something like that? *(*ONE *dies, tragically. To audience:)* Well. That kind of wraps things up. For me. As for you, what can I say? Good luck with everything. Beware. Beware. Life is tricky. You're going to lose everything. To be honest, I don't understand much about much. Get your laughs, quick, though. Life'll get you. No matter how afraid you are, you cannot be afraid enough. No matter how serious things get, they're going to get more serious still. One imagines. *(Turns to regard the falling snow.)* Snow really is a pretty remarkable thing. Even artificial snow. Snow is falling, it's starting to snow. What a great word, too: "snow." Nighty-night.

*(Lights fade to black.)*

### End of Play

# THE HARBINGERS OF TURPITUDE
## by Robin Goldwasser

## BIOGRAPHY

Robin "Goldie" Goldwasser is the "Goldwasser" half of the song-writing team Greenberg & Goldwasser, who composed the cult hit rock opera *People Are Wrong!* Ms. Goldwasser has written, directed and performed in many 24 Hour Plays over the years, including the first experiment in an evening of all-musical 24 Hour Plays. She is the founding member of The Deeply Felt Puppet Theater. For many years, she has contributed her voice as well as her puppetry to the rock band *They Might Be Giants.*

## ACKNOWLEDGMENTS

*The Harbingers of Turpitude* was originally produced by The 24 Hour Company at the Ohio Theatre in New York City on September 3, 1999. It was directed by Bennett Miller with the following cast:

| | |
|---|---|
| STEVE-O | Chris Van Strander |
| GABBY | Laura Comerford |
| LOOMIS | Jonathan Butterick |
| MISS OHIO | Leanne Littlestone |

## THE PLAYERS

STEVE-O, Group Leader
GABBY, Team Player
LOOMIS, Team Player
MISS OHIO, Theater Owner

## AUTHOR NOTE

The character name "Miss Ohio" was originally created for the performance in the Ohio Theatre in New York City. Production groups should feel free to change this character's name, as well as the reference to the Ohio Theatre later in the play, to the name of the theater in which the play is being performed.

44

# THE HARBINGERS OF TURPITUDE

*The improvisational comedy group* THE HARBINGERS OF TURPI-TUDE *take the stage. Ideally, they are dressed alike in matching t-shirts that say* THE HARBINGERS OF TURPITUDE, *but they could be just in stage-worthy street clothes: anything from nerdy to glamorous. Everyone could maybe be working a theatrical "this is who I am" look, but it's not essential.*

*On stage somewhere there's a small prop table (or better yet, a coat rack) with costume pieces on it: cowboy hat, Kaiser helmet, red glitter boa dress, rubber ducky, crutch.*

*They come into the playing area headed by group leader* STEVE-O. *He is wildly enthusiastic.* GABBY *and* LOOMIS *are somewhat lackluster but going through the motions of team spirit. They all have bottled water with them, and drink as frequently as possible, like what they do is super hard work.*

*This dialogue can be really loose. Paraphrase away, please.*

**STEVE-O.** *(Super cheerful:)* Good evening, folks! Totally awesome of you to join us here tonight! Why don't you give yourselves a round of applause! OK! Just in case you haven't hear of us, My name's Steve-o, and the intoxicatingly lovely woman to my left, sorry fellas, she's taken! My fiancé, Gabby!

**GABBY.** Hi, I'm not his fiancé. Steve-o, I'm not your fiancé…

**STEVE-O.** She's a sketch! And together, we are the improvisational comedy team: the Harbingers—

**LOOMIS.** *(With a wave:)* I'm Loomis. I'm in the group, too, Steven.

**STEVE-O.** Right. And Loomis. Can's forget Loomis. We are the Harbingers of Turpitude!

*(All strike pose, as they will every time the group's name is said.)*

And to get our first "sketch" up and running, we're going to need a little help from you, the audience! OK! Give yourselves a round of applause for helping us out in advance! Woo! OK! To start us off, we need a suggestion from the audience of a location. A location. That's a place. Anybody? We're looking for a location.

**MISS OHIO.** *(She is positively Ruth Gordon-esque.)*

*(If anyone in the audience suggests anything for real, try to call it out at the same time, so it sounds like a lot of real suggestions, but it's okay if* MISS OHIO's *is the only one.)*

A barbershop!

*(*STEVE-O *cups hand to ear, listening to suggestions. He makes up his own answers anyway.)*

**STEVE-O.** A hayloft on a small dairy farm…in upstate New York. Terrific. Okay. And we'll need a relationship…for the players…that's us. Who we are. Anyone? Just shout it out…

*(Again, listens to audience but ignores any suggestion.)*

**MISS OHIO.** You're a barbershop quartet…with one missing!

**STEVE-O.** A farmer and his wife, good, good, *(Pointing to* LOOMIS*:)* and the farmer's wife's secret lover. Okay! Awesome! Lots of possibilities there! Terrific!

*(*STEVE-O *dons straw hat from prop table.)*

**GABBY.** *(Simultaneously w/Loomis' line:)* Steve-o, that was not the suggestion.

**LOOMIS.** Are you not even going to try to do this? We could like totally do the barbershop quartet thing…like, a cappella.

**STEVE-O.** The hayloft on a small dairy farm. Upstate New York. Here we go.

*(While miming something incoherent, he speaks w/Southern accent:)*

Well, Maw, looks like the spotted heifer done gone dry agin. What more trouble kin we expect in these dark tahms?

**GABBY.** What the fuck are you doing…Paw?

**STEVE-O.** Why you silly old hen, Ah'm settin' up the still so's we can make us somma that good corn likker!

**GABBY.** Really.

**STEVE-O.** Shoot, yeah!

**GABBY.** That's great "Paw."

**STEVE-O.** Now, Maw, why don't you run along and whup me up some vittles! Wait! Who's that behind you? Is that you'rn secret lover you've been having a secret affair with which everybody in Upstate New York knows about but me?

**LOOMIS.** Steve-o, what's your problem? You want to talk about something, fine let's talk, but this is not exactly the forum—

**STEVE-O.** Steve-o? Who's Steve-o? My name's Jedediah and this here's my fucking dairy farm in Upstate New York, and yer trespassin', son! *(Starts to physically go for him in potentially fighting way.)* And the Dairy Council of Upper New York State says I got the law on my side iffen I was to kill yer bony skate-punk ass. *(Drops accent, mocking:)* Oh I'm Loomis, I'm so alternative, I'm so transgressive, I tattooed my pierced asshole—

**LOOMIS.** Dude, can you take a breath? Gabby, I am so not doing this—

**GABBY.** Hold on, Loomis. *(To audience:)* Sorry folks. We've had some recent, well, shake-ups in the old Harbingers of Turpitude Headquarters, and—

**MISS OHIO.** LaGuardia Airport!

**GABBY.** Hold on, sir. We'll get to your suggestion in a second.

**LOOMIS.** I like so totally quit.

**GABBY.** Loomis, I did not give up my Saturday night shift at Bandito's to be publicly shamed, okay? Let it go; we'll discuss it later.

**MISS OHIO.** You're my stewardess...

**GABBY.** Sir, we'll get to you later.

**MISS OHIO.** I'm a ma'am, lady.

**STEVE-O.** Um, I think I'm ready to lead the team, thank you, Gabby, my bright and precious smoldering jewel...

**GABBY.** *(Simultaneous w/*LOOMIS:*)* Fine. Fine. Lead away...

**LOOMIS.** Do it to it, Steve-"o." Take control, pally.

**STEVE-O.** Okay, we're improvising now! Woo! Okay! We just need a—

**MISS OHIO.** The bar car on the Metro North—

**STEVE-O.** —we need a location—

**MISS OHIO.** —to Mamaroneck! Ha! Riddle me that one, you bloopy-doops!

**STEVE-O.** Anybody? Anybody at all?

**MISS OHIO.** The bar car, it used to be smoking, you know? You could smoke like a chimney, no one'd say boo...Boo! Ah!

**STEVE-O.** Anybody else?

**MISS OHIO.** Oh, the times we had! Scarin' each other, sayin' Boo!

**LOOMIS.** Sir, what's you're, like, problem?

**MISS OHIO.** It's Ma'am! Actually, it's Miss!

**STEVE-O.** The top of Mount Everest. Terrific!

**GABBY.** This is not working for me anymore, Steve-o.

**STEVE-O.** And I'm the seasoned mountain guide, *(Dons Kaiser helmet:)* and I'm guiding my future wife, Gabrielle, to the top of the mountain.

**LOOMIS.** Am I invisible, here? Like, what is the dilly-o, Steven?

**STEVE-O.** Gabrielle! You must protect yourself against the brutal elements! Quick! Put this flack jacket on! *(Hands her red sequined gown with marabou trim.)*

**GABBY.** Steve-o, you wanna talk about it? Let's talk.

**LOOMIS.** Hey, like hello-o! Hello-o! Like, I'm here, too! Someone, me, gave up the 2:45 A.M. slot at Arlene Grocery to be here, so don't shut me out, okay?! Shouldn't I be part of the cabal or expedition party or something?

**STEVE-O.** Yes. And your name is Bloop.

**LOOMIS.** *(Beat.)* Bloop. Cool.

**STEVE-O.** And sadly we had to kill you and eat your flesh, Bloop. You had a game leg. It was humane, I assure you.

**GABBY.** God, Steve-o! Loomis! He didn't mean it, Loomis!

**LOOMIS.** *(Bursting into tears:)* You all…totally…suck! I quit! I quit and I'm going to kill myself!

*(Running to back of theater:)*

I quit, and I'm going to kill myself…and you're all going to watch! I'm jumping off the balcony!

*(Runs up little balcony area steps, looks over edge:)*

Okay, that's not tall enough! I'm going to jump out the back door of the Ohio Theatre and you're all going to watch!

*(He throws open latch. If it takes a while, he can ad-lib what we're going to see: his bloody corpse, his mangled limbs… He hovers whole waiting for a reaction.)*

**MISS OHIO.** *(Wandering onto the stage:)* My mother was a Metzner Girl. They were like the Zigfield Girls, only prettier!

**STEVE-O.** *(Consults secret stash of index cards hidden in helmet. Reading from cards:)* Oh, Gabrielle, now that I have you here alone, and we've sated ourselves on the flesh of our brother, I have something to tell you, my beloved…

**GABBY.** Loomis, don't jump. It's probably a big mistake.

**STEVE-O.** *(Still reading:)* With every inelegant fiber of my coarse being, with every common drop of my common blood, and with each passing second, tic-toc, tic-toc, I love you more and more…

*(Flips to next card:)*

…and more.

**MISS OHIO.** Miss Ohio, I was. From 1954-1957, undefeated! Could do it again, too. If it weren't for my sciatica.

**GABBY.** Loomis, get back in here!

**STEVE-O.** *(Still reading:)* It is with trembling hands I offer to you this: the key to my apartment, and ask you to be my official girlfriend, to share my lease, and 3 squares a day, except for I don't eat eggs. I'd have maybe an English muffin, a little juice, nothing fancy, my love…

**GABBY.** You've got that all written down?

**STEVE-O.** *(Not hearing her:)* I hate eggs.

**GABBY.** Not to nit-pick, but isn't that sort of antithetical to the long tradition of improvisation?

**LOOMIS.** I'm, like, jumping…you guys! God, I totally hate my life!

**GABBY.** Shut, like, up, Loomis, for a second! Please! Steve-o, I'm asking you, did you script an improvisation?

**STEVE-O.** No. Hey look, a rubber ducky! *(In desperation, picks up the duck from the prop table.)*

**MISS OHIO.** I am Miss Ohio! This whole damn place is mine. I don't need your handouts. I got me a goddamn theater! The Ohio Theatre! And you are all my goddamn guests!

**STEVE-O.** *(Hobbles on crutch for a second:)* Look! I broke my leg! I know, props are such a crutch! God I'm an idiot. Go out with me?

**LOOMIS.** Guys?

**GABBY.** Freaks!

**MISS OHIO.** Since you're all my goddamn guests…let's dance!

> *(Dance music starts up.)*

## Ending #1

**STEVE-O.** Stop the music!

> *(Music stops.)*

It is time to take poison and die!

> *(Collective eye-rolling.)*

We don't do it often, but when the Harbingers of Turpitude come to logger-heads, group suicide is the only way to resolve our differences.

> *(Everyone takes a little vial of something from their pocket.)*
> *(They swallow the contents.)*
> *(They bleed from the mouth, clutch their stomach, convulse, and die…)*
> *(They are still for some beats, then hop to their feet jolly and clapping and laughing.)*

**ALL.** The Harbingers of Turpitude!: Kicking ass in all directions!

> *(They stop, freeze, then rewind in fast motion, un-clapping, un-dying, un-taking poison, back to where ending #1 began.)*
> *(Music starts up again.)*

## Ending #2

**STEVE-O.** Stop the music!

> *(Music stops.)*

It is time to take poison and die!

> *(Collective eye-rolling.)*

We don't do it often, but when the Harbingers of Turpitude come to logger-heads, group suicide is the only way to resolve our differences.

> *(Everyone takes a big horse pill [Alka-Seltzer?] from their pocket.)*
> *(They pop it in their mouth, maybe take a sip of water.)*
> *(They foam at the mouth, clutch their throats, convulse, and die.)*
> *(They are still for some beats, then hop to their feet jolly and clapping and laughing.)*

**ALL.** The Harbingers of Turpitude!: Feel our total rage!

*(They stop, freeze, then rewind in fast motion, un-clapping, un-dying, un-taking poison, back to where ending #2 began.)*

*(Music starts up again.)*

## Ending #3

**STEVE-O.** Stop the music!

*(Music stops.)*

It is time to take hands and hug!

*(Collective eye-rolling.)*

We don't do it often, but when the Harbingers of Turpitude come to loggerheads, a big group hug is the only way to resolve our differences.

*(The Harbingers take each others hands.)*

**STEVE-O.** Uh, I said Group hug, folks. That's right, you too, don't be shy! I want everyone in this theater holding hands! Yeah! Yeah! Do it! Everybody! Hold hands! That's right, reach behind you, reach across the aisle, good, good… Everyone holding hands? All right!

**ALL.** The Harbingers of Turpitude: We're all about love!

*(Music starts up again.)*

*(They clap with hands above their heads, jump up and down wildly and congratulate each other with high fives and whoops.)*

### *The Like, Total End*

# TOCCATA AND FUGUE
## by Tina Howe

**Required royalties must be paid every time this play is performed before any audience, whether or not it is presented for profit and whether or not admission is charged.** Inquiries concerning rights, including stock and amateur performance rights, you must contact:

**Playscripts, Inc.**

website:  www.playscripts.com
email:    info@playscripts.com
phone:    1-866-NEW-PLAY (639-7529)

Inquiries concerning all other rights should be addressed to the author's agent: Thomas Pearson, ICM, 825 Eighth Avenue, 26th Floor, New York, NY 10019.

## BIOGRAPHY

Tina Howe's best known plays include *Birth and After Birth*, *Museum*, *The Art of Dining*, *Painting Churches*, *Coastal Disturbances* and *Pride's Crossing*. Among her many awards are an Obie, a Guggenheim, a New York Drama Critics' Circle Award, a Tony nomination, a Pulitzer finalist twice and a couple of honorary degrees. Grove Press recently published her translations of Eugène Ionesco's *The Bald Soprano* and *The Lesson*. She has been a Visiting Professor of Play-writing at Hunter College since 1990. Her most recent play, *Chasing Manet* opened at Primary Stages in spring of 2009.

## ACKNOWLEDGMENTS

*Toccata and Fugue* was originally produced by The 24 Hour Company at The American Airlines Theatre as part of *The 24 Hour Plays on Broadway* on October 23, 2006. It was directed by Josie Rourke with the following cast:

SIR HUMPHREY
WAGG-THORNTON.........................................Wallace Shawn
CHARLOTTE........................................................Catherine Tate
CONCETTA.....................................Elizabeth Berkley-Lauren
TOTO ................................................................... John Linnell

## CAST OF CHARACTERS

SIR HUMPHREY WAGG THORNTON, a world-famous organist suffering from stage fright
CHARLOTTE, Sir Humphrey's daughter
CONCETTA, Toto's sister
TOTO, his long-suffering mute French servant who plays the accordion

## TIME

The present.

## SETTING

The sitting room of an elegant English townhouse, circa 1910. It's most striking feature is an organ at one end of the room.

# Toccata and Fugue

*The play begins in darkness. We hear an accordion playing an exceedingly sad rendition of "La Vie en Rose." Still in darkness we hear* SIR HUM-PHREY's *voice.*

**SIR HUMPHREY.** Sadder, Toto…sadder. *(With a bad French accent:)* Plus triste!

*(Lights rise and we see a very depressed* SIR HUMPHREY *stretched out on the sofa, covered with a blanket.* TOTO, *his mute French servant is playing the accordion. As he plays…)*

*(Author's note:* SIR HUMPHREY *might have an English accent, but doesn't have to.* CHARLOTTE *has an English accent.* CONCETTA *has a Hispanic accent.* TOTO *is mute.)*

**SIR HUMPHREY.** Toto, I didn't rescue you from the bowels of the Paris metro to cheer me up! I want pathos! I want tristesse! I want tears! How do you say en Francais? *(Mimes weeping:)* Des larmes… Beaucoup de larmes… Wash me away in a river of larmes!

*(*TOTO *starts playing something sadder.)*

**SIR HUMPHREY.** *(In an orgy of self pity:)* Ahh Toto! To think I was once one of the greatest organists in the world—knighted by Queen Elizabeth herself…and look at me now…

**CHARLOTTE.** *(Running into the room:)* Father, there you are! I was looking for you everywhere! In the library, the garden, the stables, the potting shed… I should have known you'd be holed up in here with Toto. Really Father, when one thinks of your stature…

**SIR HUMPHREY.** "Thinks"? One doesn't "think" here at Heartbreak House, one suffers!

**CHARLOTTE.** Speak for yourself. *(Lowering her voice:)* I've come to tell you I've fallen in love.

**SIR HUMPHREY.** What's that you said? "Fallen in love"? YOU? In LOVE?

**CHARLOTTE.** Play us a love song Toto! Something delirious!

*(*TOTO *obliges.* CHARLOTTE *starts spinning around the room.)*

**SIR HUMPHREY.** How dare you dance in my presence? You know the rules in this house.

**CHARLOTTE.** *(Continuing to dance:)* Rules, fools, tools, ghouls!

**SIR HUMPHREY.** Toto, I order you to stop that sickening music, toute suite! *(Pointing to the door:)* Allez-vous en before I strangle you to death! Go! Salot!

*(TOTO rushes out of the room. Dead silence.)*

**CHARLOTTE.** Father, that's no way to talk to the help. I know you're suffering, but you should make an effort to be nicer to Toto...

**SIR HUMPHREY.** *(Trying to drown her out:)* Ba ba ba ba ba ba ba ba ba ba ba ba ba *(Etc.)*

**CHARLOTTE.** He's had his disappointments too. Born mute, separated from his twin sister at birth, an alcoholic at the age of 12...in and out of reform schools...

*(TOTO starts to play a sad tune way off stage.)*

**CHARLOTTE.** Just listen to the poor man, he's in worse shape than you are.

**SIR HUMPHREY.** My dear Charlotte, let me ask you a simple question: Which is a worse fate—to fall from a great height or to fall from no height at all?

*(Silence as he waits for an answer.)*

**SIR HUMPHREY.** Toto went from being a beggar in the Paris metro to playing for me for 30 pounds a week! That's hardly a fall! Whereas I went from being the greatest organist...in the world...to getting such a titanic case of stage fright in Mexico City I could never perform again. Why it happened there I'll never know, but that was the end for me... *(Rises and starts pacing around the room.)* No more mounting the steps to the organ loft... No more pulling out those dainty stops, no more dancing on the slatted pedals... No more Bach passacaglias in Thomas Kirche or Handel concertos in Kings College, no more... *(Long pause.)* sound... That enormous...floodlit sound that sent the lambs and apostles jitterbugging right out of their stained glass windows! Now I'm left with this...this...travesty...this...tinny...wheezing death! *(Yelling offstage:)* Play me a sad tune, Toto! It's the l'heure bleu!

*(There's a sexy lighting change.)*

*(TOTO plays a sad tune offstage. There's a slight pause.)*

**CHARLOTTE.** *(Suddenly very cheerful:)* So...don't you want to hear who I've fallen in love with?

**SIR HUMPHREY.** Not particularly. You have appalling taste in men.

**CHARLOTTE.** Well, Father, I have good news for you. I've finally seen the light.

**SIR HUMPHREY.** You've met a real man?

**CHARLOTTE.** Not exactly.

**SIR HUMPHREY.** He's either real or not.

**CHARLOTTE.** You couldn't call him...a real man.

**SIR HUMPHREY.** A fake man, then?

**CHARLOTTE.** No.

**SIR HUMPHREY.** A dead man?

**CHARLOTTE.** Thanks a lot!

**SIR HUMPHREY.** What is he then?

*(CHARLOTTE outlines a female shape with her hands.)*

**SIR HUMPHREY.** Let's see… A sailor?

*(CHARLOTTE nods no and makes the outline again.)*

**SIR HUMPHREY.** A jockey?

*(CHARLOTTE nods no and makes the outline even more provocative.)*

**SIR HUMPHREY.** *(Triumphant:)* A penguin!

**CHARLOTTE.** FATHER, WHAT'S WRONG WITH YOU? YOU'RE SO OUT OF TOUCH WITH REALITY, YOU DON'T EVEN RECOGNIZE THE SHAPE OF A WOMAN!!!

**SIR HUMPHREY.** *(Confused:)* A woman?

**CHARLOTTE.** Yes, a woman! She's waiting right outside.

*(TOTO starts playing a sexy tune off stage.)*

**CHARLOTTE.** And you'll never guess who she is!

**SIR HUMPHREY.** Well, how could I possibly guess I don't know any…

*(An awkward pause.)*

**CHARLOTTE.** Women. Go on, you can say it.

**SIR HUMPHREY.** *(Barely audible:)* Women.

**CHARLOTTE.** Very good.

**SIR HUMPHREY.** You say there's a…woman? In our house? In… Heartbreak House? It's been so long… I don't even remember what a…what a…

**CHARLOTTE.** Woman…

**SIR HUMPHREY.** Looks like.

**CHARLOTTE.** Come on, Mother didn't leave you that long ago… *(Pause.)* How long has it been?

**SIR HUMPHREY.** *(As if in a dream:)* A woman…

**CHARLOTTE.** And not just any woman, but Toto's sister!

**SIR HUMPHREY.** A woman…

**CHARLOTTE.** The twin he was separated from at birth… She found him through the internet.

**SIR HUMPHREY.** A woman…

**CHARLOTTE.** Concetta! Concetta is waiting outside! *(Pause, then yelling offstage to TOTO:)* I SAID, CONCETTA IS WAITING OUTSIDE!

*(TOTO enters and plays a fanfare. There's a knock on the door.)*

**SIR HUMPHREY.** Good grief, someone's at the door! Who could it be?

**CHARLOTTE.** Well, answer it and see.

**SIR HUMPHREY.** But I haven't answered the door since your mother left. *(The knocking becomes more insistent.)*

**CHARLOTTE.** *(In a stage whisper:)* Go on, you can do it.

*(*SIR HUMPHREY *goes to the door and opens it.* CONCETTA, *a phenomenally beautiful blonde enters carrying a bottle of Gran Centenario Tequila. No one moves.)*

**CHARLOTTE / SIR HUMPHREY / TOTO.** Baby! Jesus Christ! *(Plays a joyful chord.)*

**CONCETTA.** *(Gaping at* SIR HUMPHREY, *in a Mexican accent:)* Señor Humphrey Wagg-Thornton!

**SIR HUMPHREY.** My oh my oh my oh my oh my oh my...

**CONCETTA.** Is it really you?

**SIR HUMPHREY.** I have no idea.

**CONCETTA.** Ever since I heard you play Bach's *Passacaglia and Fugue* in A minor in Mexico City, I have been determined to find you. Here, I brought you this.

*(She hands him the bottle of tequila which he puts somewhere.)*

**SIR HUMPHREY.** Did you say...Mexico City?

**CONCETTA.** Sí Señor.

**SIR HUMPHREY.** You were there?

**CONCETTA.** Sí, sí. It's where I grew up. When my mother discovered Toto was mute, she thought he'd been touched by the devil, so she left him in the street and ran away with me to Mexico.

*(*TOTO *plays a fitting tune.)*

**CHARLOTTE.** Isn't she...fabulous? Isn't she the most fabulous person you've ever seen? Look at her! Just look at her!

**CONCETTA.** That is where I heard you play... You played so beautifully in our Eglesia Santa Maria de le Croce I thought my heart would stop. In fact, it did stop. Perhaps you remember the women screaming when I fell to the floor and was carried out... Even I remember their cries though I was almost dead... *(She launches into some serious Spanish wailing, as...)*

**SIR HUMPHREY.** Yes, yes...it's coming back...those screams as I was playing... I heard all this wailing and suddenly I knew what had happened... The faithful were raising their voices against me! Against my pride. I was the one demanding to be worshipped! Light was pouring from my hands! I was the god! I needed to be punished... And so I never played again.

**CONCETTA.** No, no, Señor...it was me—melting at your beautiful music. Play for me again, I am stronger now, I won't faint. There will be no wailing. Only rejoicing. I promise you.

**CHARLOTTE.** *(Taking* SIR HUMPHREY's *arm and leading him towards the organ:)* Come on, Father, it's not nice to keep a woman waiting. Especially a woman as beautiful as my Concetta!

**SIR HUMPHREY.** *(Sitting on the organ bench:)* A woman... *(With a twinkle in his eye:)* My new daughter in law. Who would have thought!

**CONCETTA.** Play for me, Señor Humphrey Wagg-Thornton! Let the saints and sinners rejoice once more!

*(*SIR HUMPHREY *settles down and plays Bach's thundering "Passacaglia and Fugue" in A minor.* CHARLOTTE, CONCETTA, *and* TOTO *listen, their arms wrapped around each other.)*

## End of Play

# THE BLIZZARD
## by David Ives

# BIOGRAPHY

David Ives is probably best known for his evenings of one-acts, collected as *All in the Timing* (Vintage Books) and *Time Flies* (Grove Press). His full-length work to date has been collected in *Polish Joke and Other Plays* (Grove). He is also the author of two young-adult novels, *Monsieur Eek* and *Scrib*. He lives in New York City with his wife, Martha.

# ACKNOWLEDGMENTS

*The Blizzard* was originally produced by The 24 Hour Company at The American Airlines Theatre as part of *The 24 Hour Plays on Broadway* on October 23, 2006. It was directed by Bennett Miller with the following cast:

| | |
|---|---|
| JENNY | Anna Paquin |
| NEIL | Fisher Stevens |
| SALIM | Aasif Mandvi |
| NATASHA | Gaby Hoffman |

# CAST OF CHARACTERS

JENNY
NEIL
SALIM
NATASHA

*This play is for Walter Bobbie.*

# THE BLIZZARD

*A country house, toward evening. Cold winter light outside. Throughout the play, the lights gradually dim around center stage to nighttime. At curtain,* JENNY *is onstage alone.*

**JENNY.** *(Calls:)* Neil? —Neil? —*Neil!*

*(*NEIL *enters.)*

**NEIL.** It's still coming down. Some of those drifts are a yard deep already. What's the matter?

**JENNY.** Nothing. I just wondered what happened to you.

**NEIL.** Got scared, huh?

**JENNY.** No, I wasn't *scared.* The food's all ready. Do you really think they'll make it up here in this?

**NEIL.** Joe's got those new chains on the car. The ones that Sandy made him fork out for? Just what you'd expect from Miss Rationality.

**JENNY.** Right. Mr. *List Maker.* Mr. My-Pencils-Have-To-Be-Laid-Out-In-The-Right-Order-On-My-Desk. No, you're not rational. Sandy is rational.

**NEIL.** What about the TV?

**JENNY.** Nothing. Not a thing.

**NEIL.** The electricity's on. You'd think with a satellite dish we'd pick up *some*thing.

**JENNY.** The telephone's still out.

**NEIL.** They've probably been trying us on their cell since they left the city.

**JENNY.** There's no radio either.

**NEIL.** No *radio?*

**JENNY.** Isn't it *great?* It's just like an Agatha Christie.

**NEIL.** Thanks for that. I'm still not used to it. Being so remote. Nature's always scared the living hell out of me. Now I'm living in it. Or visiting it on weekends, anyway. You know I saw a bat flapping around out there? I didn't know there were bats in snowstorms. No *radio?*

The world could be ending out there, for Christ's sake. And we'd be the last ones to hear about it. No *radio…*

**JENNY.** We have no radio and a beautiful blizzard and a house and woods and a mountain that are all ours.

**NEIL.** All ours in 29 years and three months.

**JENNY.** I kind of wish they weren't coming up tonight. It's so cozy. I wouldn't mind curling up with a book.

**NEIL.** I wish you hadn't said "Agatha Christie."

61

**JENNY.** You inflict *Torturama* One, Two and Three on people and I can't say "Agatha Christie"?

**NEIL.** Those are movies, not a real house in the middle of the real country with the lines down. And *Torturama* paid for our little mansion on a hill, babe.

**JENNY.** You know what it is about murder mysteries? No, listen. I think the reason people like murder mysteries is that, in a murder mystery, everything is *significant*. The people in murder mysteries are living in a *significant world*. A world where everything is there for a reason. Even before the murder's happened, you know that one is going to happen and you know that everything is a *clue*. Or rather, you know that some things are clues and some things are just obfuscation, they're snow. And you know that everybody has a secret of some kind. A secret that's like a soul. Murder mysteries are religious, in a way. Don't laugh. They're like the way you feel it when you're in love. When everything's in a special light. They're a couple of hours of everything *meaning* something, for God's sake. And then they're over and you're back to your old life, to real life. To mortgages and pork loin and potatoes and making a rhubarb pie.

**NEIL.** Real life doesn't feel like it means something these days?

**JENNY.** Sure it does. I'm just saying…well, don't we all wish for that in real life? One of those moments when everything feels charged with meaning? When the air is electric?

**NEIL.** Well here's your opportunity. Listen, we're probably going to be totally snowed in. Why don't we all do something different this weekend.

**JENNY.** Different, what does different mean?

**NEIL.** I don't know. Something unusual. Something unexpected. Not you and Sandy holing yourself up in the kitchen and talking about whatever you talk about, not me and Joe sitting around talking about Mom and Dad and what happened in the third grade. Not the usual pour a glass of Jack Daniels, bullshit bullshit bullshit, what've you guys been doing, go in to dinner and break out the Margaux '01, have you seen any movies, did you catch that episode of blah blah blah. I don't know, something we've never done before, or let's talk about something we've never talked about before. Anything, instead of all the things we usually talk about.

**JENNY.** Okay. Something unusual. It's a deal.

**SALIM.** *(Off-Stage:)* Hello—? Neil?

**NEIL.** There they are.

*(SALIM and NATASHA enter. SALIM carries a black plastic valise.)*

**SALIM.** Hello! Neil and Jenny, right? Sorry for the cold hand, I'm freezing. God, you're just like Joe and Sandy described you. I can't believe I'm finally meeting you, Neil. I am such a fan of *Torturama*. All of them. Natasha can't watch them, herself. Natasha is squeamish.

**NEIL.** I'm sorry, I don't understand…

**SALIM.** Salim. And Natasha.

**NATASHA.** *(Who has a trace of a foreign accent:)* Hello. I'm so happy to en-counter you at last. And you, Jenny, you are just as beautiful as Sandy told me. You are exquisite.

**SALIM.** And God, what a place up here! But so remote! Wow! We brought this for you. Here.

> *(Holds up the black valise.)*

A little housewarming gift.

**NEIL.** Whoa, whoa, whoa. I'm sorry, maybe there's been a mistake…

**SALIM.** I mean, this is the place, isn't it? You're Neil and Jenny? Oh, right, right. *Where are Joe and Sandy.* Middle of a snowstorm. Two strange people walk in. You're spooked. Totally natural. Natasha?

**NATASHA.** Joe and Sandy couldn't make it, so they sent us instead.

**NEIL.** They sent you instead. Wait a minute. They sent *you* instead…

**SALIM.** They caught some kind of bug. God, Joe and Sandy have been tell-ing us all about you two for I don't know how long.

**NATASHA.** A long time.

**SALIM.** A very long time.

**NEIL.** I don't think Joe and Sandy ever mentioned knowing a, I'm sorry…

**SALIM.** Salim.

**NEIL.** A Salim and a Natasha.

**SALIM.** You've been out of touch with your brother for too long, brother. They were really broken up they couldn't make it tonight. I'd say call them up and ask them but hey, are your cell phones as down as ours up here?

**JENNY.** How do you know Joe and Sandy?

**SALIM.** *(The black valise:)* You know what's in here? Just for showing us your hospitality? It's this new tequila, a hundred bucks a bottle. Olé, right? Let's support those oppressed brothers churning this stuff out for ten cents a day. Neil, you want to pour?

**JENNY.** You didn't answer me.

**NATASHA.** How do we know Joe and Sandy.

**SALIM.** How do we know Joe and Sandy. How do we know them, Natasha?

**NATASHA.** Intimately.

**SALIM.** Intimately. Good word. We know them intimately.

**JENNY.** Neil… *Neil…*

**NEIL.** Look, I'm very sorry, but I'm going to have to ask you to leave.

**SALIM.** To leave? But…okay, I get it, I get it, you want some kind of proof that we're not just what…

**NATASHA.** Imposters.

**SALIM.** Imposters. Ten points, Natasha. We're not imposters! We're the real thing! I'm sorry if I'm coming on kind of strong, it's my personality, you know what I mean? God, how do you prove that you know somebody? Let's see. Where do I start? Do I start with Joe or Sandy? You know she made him get these hotshot snow chains for the car. That is so Sandy. No imagination, but always thinking ahead. So *rational.*

> *(Pause.)*

Listen. Listen, I'm sorry we barged in on you like this. Maybe we should leave, but…hey, are you really going to turn two freezing strangers back out into the storm? Neil, you're the guy who inflicted *Torturama* on the world, more killings per square frame than any movie in history. You're pouring blood in the aisles, man. Don't tell me you're scared. What are you scared of? What am I going to do to you, huh? If I was going to do something to you I'd've done it already, wouldn't I?

> *(Pause.)*

So do we leave? Or do we stay? Aw, have a heart, Neil.

**NEIL.** Well, we can't turn you out in this weather…

**JENNY.** Turn them out, Neil.

**NEIL.** Honey, I…

**JENNY.** Turn them out.

**NEIL.** It's a blizzard out there, honey.

**SALIM.** Your wife is so sweet. Really. She is a doll.

**NATASHA.** You know, with so much snow, it's like we're in a murder mystery here.

**SALIM.** Natasha adores Agatha Christie. You know what I hate about murder mysteries? It's that everybody in them's got a secret. People don't have secrets. People are open books. I don't know you personally, Neil, but just looking at you I'd say you're probably the kind of guy who makes lists, for example. Lines his pencils up on the desk. Likes things neat and tidy. Am I right? A Jack Daniels before dinner kinda guy. You're not the kind of guy who, what, secretly worked for the CIA once upon a time, you're not a guy with a secret history of killing people, I mean *really* killing people, off screen, you don't have any real blood on your hands. You're in the entertainment industry. You have nothing to hide.

**JENNY.** Send them away, Neil.

**SALIM.** And Jenny, she probably made her usual dinner for tonight, let's see what would it be, pork loin and some kind of special potato recipe and a cherry-rhubarb pie for dessert. The perfect American housewife. Nothing to conceal. I'm sorry, I'm sorry, there's that personality of mine again. I'm brash. I'm insensitive. I'm loud. Call me American.

**NEIL.** You know I have a gun in the house.

**SALIM.** Oh, that's rich. What a liar! "I have a gun in the house." Right. That's so cute. This isn't a movie, this is *real life,* Neil. And I'm your brother for the night. I'm a stand-in for Joe. Remember me? Your brother?

**JENNY.** Where are Joe and Sandy?

**SALIM.** They're very sick in bed is where they are.

**JENNY.** What have you done with them?

**SALIM.** They can't move is what they are. Aren't I your brother? Neil? Come on.

(*He puts his arm around* NEIL's *waist.*)

Am I your brother?

**NEIL.** Sure…

**SALIM.** Am I your brother? Am I your brother? Am I your brother?

**NEIL.** You're my brother.

**SALIM.** There you see? How hard was that? Now we can talk about all those kids we used to beat up in third grade. Just like old times. Well, brother, what do you say? We're here for the duration. You gonna play the good host here or what?

**NEIL.** Shall we go in to dinner?

**SALIM.** Attaboy!

(SALIM *pushes* NEIL *out and follows him off.*)

**NATASHA.** You know what I love about murder mysteries? Is that everything in them seems to mean something. The people in murder mysteries are living in a significant world. Everything holding its breath. Waiting. The air is electric. And then, bang, it happens. The irrevocable. Whatever that is. Changing everything. It's a kind of poetry. To me, it's almost a religious feeling.

**JENNY.** I don't want any more fucking significance. I don't want it. I don't want it.

**NATASHA.** (*Embraces* JENNY.) Poor Jenny. Afraid over nothing. Why? Why?

**JENNY.** You have the wrong people.

**NATASHA.** You're the right people. You're Neil and Jenny. We're just here for dinner with you. And you have nothing to be afraid of. Really. Absolutely nothing.

**JENNY.** (*Calls out:*) Neil…? *Neil…?*

**NATASHA.** Absolutely nothing…

(*The lights fade.*)

### *End of Play*

# SPACE
## by Laura Jacqmin

## BIOGRAPHY

Laura Jacqmin is a Chicago-based playwright, raised in Cleveland, Ohio. She is a resident playwright at Chicago Dramatists, a founding ensemble member of At Play Productions, and the winner of the 2008 Wasserstein Prize (a $25,000 award for emerging female playwrights) for *and when we awoke there was light and light*. Her plays have been produced and developed by Chicago Dramatists, Ars Nova, Victory Gardens Theater, Second Stage Theatre, Steppenwolf Theatre Company, Northlight Theatre, the Contemporary American Theater Festival, The 24 Hour Plays: Old Vic/New Voices at the Atlantic Theater, and the inaugural NNPN's University Playwrights Workshop at the National Center for New Plays at Stanford University, among others. Her play *Happyslap* was a winner of Aurora Theatre Company's 2007 Global Age Project; her play *and when we awoke there was light and light* is a 2009 winner of the same award. Ms. Jacqmin earned a BA from Yale, an MFA in playwriting from Ohio University, and has been a regular freelance contributor to *The Onion A.V. Club* and chicago.decider.com.

## ACKNOWLEDGMENTS

*Space* was originally produced by The 24 Hour Company in association with At Play Productions at The Atlantic Theater on the set of *Parlour Song* in New York City on March 17, 2008. It was directed by Colette Robert and featured the following cast:

| | |
|---|---|
| SAM | Zoe Perry |
| IRINA | Sarah Eliana Bisman |
| ALICE | Jessica Walter |

## CAST OF CHARACTERS

SAM, 20s. Tomboy. Skinny mini. In Nome.

IRINA, 20s-30s. Russian. Not so skinny mini. In Russia.

ALICE, telegraph operator and ultra-female Alaskan. So proper. So prim. 30s-50s.

## SET

Nome, Alaska. Plus another place.

## PRODUCTION NOTES

Throughout the course of the play, Sam and Irina speak into walkie-talkies. The volume should be dialed all the way down so that we do not hear their voices through the walkies—just the beep when the button is released at the end of each chunk of dialogue. The effect should be much like the STOP in a telegram that occurs after each sentence. Please note, the beeps should not punctuate every sentence; nor should they only come at the very end of a speech, but instead, should be interspersed throughout.

At the end of the play, the volume should be dialed all the way up so that Sam's voice can only be heard as filtered through the walkie-talkie.

# SPACE

SAM *and* IRINA, *not close to each other, each with a walkie-talkie. When they speak, they hold the yellow button to talk. When they release the yellow button, there is an automatic beep.* ALICE *is here too, apart. When she speaks, she addresses the audience.*

**SAM.** So here I am in Alaska.

Nome. Which starts with an N, not a GN, as in: "garden."

Population: 3,950. In other words, not that many.

Nome is the closest you can possibly get to Russia and still be in the non-continental United States.

And I need you to understand why I'm in Alaska.

**IRINA.** I can't quite hear you because I'm about to go into space.

We're launching soon.

We're starting the countdown.

4.

3.

2.

1.

Is what it will sound like.

Blast-off!

Which won't sound like the word itself, but like: ka-schpoooooooooooom.

Phoooooooooo.

**SAM.** Why are you going to space?

**IRINA.** We're putting together a giant robot.

**SAM.** What does it do?

**IRINA.** It slowly lifts its hand to its mouth. Over and over again. Hand to mouth. Down to the waist. And back up again.

And it breathes.

**SAM.** Where will it live?

**IRINA.** Outside the station. In the cold of space.

**SAM.** It's not allowed inside, with everyone else?

**IRINA.** It wouldn't fit.

And besides.

It's not quite human.

**ALICE.** Dear new next door neighbor.

This is Alice: the one who owns the big red cabin about four miles away from you, and who runs the town telegraph machine.

71

Thank you for the loaf of banana bread and the kind thank-you note for helping you to loft your food supply into the big Betula Neoalaskana tree on your property.

I still think the Tsuga Mertensiana would have been a better choice, but you'll figure that out when a bear comes sniffing around.

However, and I say this as simply and honestly as I know how, I must ask you to cease all communication with me from this point forward.

**IRINA.** How is Alaska?

**SAM.** Overrun with the oversized creatures of this world.
You can find:
Dall-sheep.
Buffalo.
Musk oxen.
Bieber.
Reindeers.
Ram.
And, obviously, moose. You must beware of moose.

    *(Beat.)*

This place is very vast and I'm very alone.
How's space?

**IRINA.** Almost-space.
It's beautiful. We're checking the oxygen tanks. We're writing heartfelt letters to our families, who we may never see again. We're testing our moon-boots.

**SAM.** What do you see out your window?

**IRINA.** Green. Green and asphalt and low, gray sky as far as the eye can see.
What do you see out your window?

**SAM.** Blue. Alaskan blue. A clearer, more frozen blue than I've ever seen before.
Sandwiched between the Chukchi Sea and Norton Sound.

    *(Beat.)*

What does space sound like?

**IRINA.** It sounds like this:

    *(IRINA presses the button of her walkie and blows into it: from the side, so that we can see what she's doing. The noise comes over the other walkie: a low whoosh.)*

**SAM.** It sounds beautiful.

**ALICE.** Nome is a small town. Everybody knows everybody in Nome. Some people have been here since the great diphtheria epidemic of 1925, when sled dogs ran shipments of life-saving serum all the way up from Anchorage.
We rely on our neighbors in Nome.

And you and I?

Well.

There we were, winter-proofing your cabin. Picking out thermometers in town. Me teaching you to burn your used toilet paper while out hiking.

Two women, unmarried, in the Alaskan tundra.

Neighbors. Friends, perhaps.

I thought I would loan you my favorite book: "Catch and Release: A Guide to Alaska Men."

I thought I could maybe rely on you.

**IRINA.** You could come with me.

**SAM.** Into space?

I couldn't.

The moon boots don't fit me.

And I don't understand the astronaut language. I don't know the first thing about robot construction.

**IRINA.** You apply for special papers. And then it doesn't matter about the words or the robots or the boots, because I'll help you. We'll take walks on the green grass and the dark asphalt under the low, gray sky and we can snack on freeze-dried food.

Wearing regular shoes.

And regular clothes.

No helmets.

No ventilators or oxygen tanks.

Just cold, crisp atmosphere.

**SAM.** I want to.

**IRINA.** You do?

**SAM.** I do.

**ALICE.** Everybody said that once we got an airport and satellite Internet, nobody would want to send telegrams anymore.

But people like telegrams.

They need telegrams.

They dream of the capital letters and the full stops and the tick, tick, tick of the machine.

So I've kept my telegraph. And on it, I receive all the messages that folks who aren't from Nome, Alaska, send this town's way.

I intercepted your message.

Translated, from the Russian, so that you can understand.

**SAM.** What are you writing in your heartfelt letter to your family? To the people you care for most?

**IRINA.** Dear.

Dear, dear, dear, dear, dear.

Dear you.

**SAM.** Is the whole thing a greeting?

**IRINA.** It will be a very long time before we get to say hello to each other again.

Months.

Hundreds upon hundreds of days.

Thousands upon thousands of hours.

**SAM.** Stop it.

**IRINA.** Millions upon millions of minutes.

**SAM.** I can't bear it.

**IRINA.** You can.

**SAM.** I can't remember your face.

**IRINA.** It looks like a face.

**SAM.** Your neck.

**IRINA.** Is still a neck.

**SAM.** Your whole body.

**IRINA.** Is alive and well, being body-like.

**SAM.** In space.

Far away.

**IRINA.** Not so far away.

**SAM.** Terribly, horribly far away.

**IRINA.** Come here if it's so far.

**SAM.** I can't.

**IRINA.** Come here!

**SAM.** We can't speak anymore.

That's why I'm calling.

We shouldn't even talk.

It's too gross. I can't do it and I'm getting frostbite and we can't just row back and forth every day between the place you live and the place I live.

Or hike the Bering Strait, which doesn't even exist anymore.

There's just no way to do it.

**ALICE.** I've enclosed your telegram. I wanted to deliver it in person because I felt it vital that you received my message at the same time.

Your visa appeal has been denied.

No fiancée visa will be granted for Irina Ialovskii to bring Samantha Hallenstein to the city of Provideniya at the easternmost tip of the Russian continent, sandwiched between the Chukchi Sea and Norton Sound. The Russian consulate cannot recognize this petition.

**SAM.** So this is what I'm saying.

This is how it's going to be.

We have to be done. And we'll never talk again.

Because.

I'm in Nome, Alaska. The closest you can possibly get to Russia and still be in the non-continental United States.

And it's not close enough.

>    (*Beat.*)

**IRINA.** 4.

3.

2.

1.

Blast-off.

>    (*IRINA puts her walkie-talkie down on the stage, leaving it turned on, and fades off, away.*)

**ALICE.** What I suppose I'm trying to say is, Sam, you just don't fit.

I cannot invite you inside.

You are not quite human. You must stay out.

And out in Nome, Alaska, is a cold, empty place to be.

Respectfully, your neighbor. Alice.

>    (*ALICE also fades away. SAM is alone. She begins the robot ritual: raising and lowering her hand to her mouth. Slowly, she raises the walkie-talkie to her mouth. She pushes the button and blows into it, lightly: a low whoosh comes from the abandoned walkie. She lowers the walkie to her waist. She lifts it, pushes the button, blows into it. Lowers it. Lifts it, speaks into it.*)

**SAM.** Hello?

Let me in, please.

Let me in.

## *End of Play*

# THE FREELANCERS
## by Lucy Kirkwood

## BIOGRAPHY

Lucy Kirkwood is an East London born playwright. She won the PMA award in 2006. She is a writer on the Channel 4 programme *Skins* and is currently resident writer at Clean Break theatre company. Her first full professional production, *Tinderbox*, was directed by Josie Rourke and performed at the Bush Theatre, London, in 2008. Her adaptation of Henrik Ibsen's *Hedda Gabler*, entitled *Hedda*, was directed by Carrie Cracknell and performed at the Gate Theatre later that year. She is currently working on a Sloan commission for the Manhattan Theatre Club and a full-length one-woman show for Clean Break, as well as various television and film projects.

## ACKNOWLEDGMENTS

*The Freelancers* was originally produced by Anna Dawson, Caroline Dyott, Henry Filloux-Bennett, Alex Segal, Charlotte Sutton, Tara Wilkinson, and Chantelle Stayings with Old Vic New Voices and The 24 Hour Company at The Old Vic on the set of *Speed-the-Plow* in London on March 30, 2008. It was directed by Jonny Humphreys and featured the following cast:

JOSIE ....................................................................... Lorna Beckett
VOICE / GIDEON ...................................... Joseph Radcliffe
MARGERY ............................................................ Daisy Brydon
TERENCE ............................................................ Ciaran Owens

## CAST OF CHARACTERS

JOSIE
VOICE / GIDEON
MARGERY
TERENCE

# THE FREELANCERS

*A modern flat. Entirely empty except for one door-stop shaped like a West Highland Terrier in the middle of the room.*

*JOSIE enters in a rush, carrying a hand-bag and talking on her mobile.*

**JOSIE.** ...no Mum, you haven't won the Nigerian lottery...because you haven't...because it's a scam... Mum don't—what? I'm fine. I'm fine. I'm—

*(As she speaks she pulls off her coat. Without looking she hangs it on the hat-stand on which she always hangs her coat.)*

*(Except the hat-stand isn't there today. In fact, almost nothing of what was there when she left the flat this morning is there now. Except for the door-stop.)*

*(So when she reaches out to hang up her coat, it drops to the floor.)*

*(JOSIE turns and stares at it.)*

**JOSIE.** Mum? I'm going to have to call you back.

*(She hangs up, then looks round for the first time and takes in the emptiness of the space. She's numb with incomprehension. Then she turns and spots the door-stop. She stares at it.)*

**JOSIE.** I'm going to fucking kill him.

*(JOSIE takes out her mobile and dials. The call is answered.)*

**JOSIE.** Greg? Greg, don't—yes it's me. Me. Josie. Josie Simmons. Yes, *that* Josie. Your ex-fiancé. Yes I know I sound perturbed. That's because I am *perturbed*, Greg. Where are you? What bar? It's very noisy, can you—I said it's VERY NOISY, can you—

Who's that? What do you mean who? Who's talking to you?

Someone just asked if you wanted a Sambuca, who was it?

Jeff Goldblum? As in...Jeff Goldblum?

You're a telemarketer from Penge, Greg! Where the fuck did you meet Jeff Goldblum?

What do you mean, "he's a mate"? How is Jeff Goldblum your mate? We went out for five years Greg, and not once in that time did you ever once mention Jeff fucking Goldblum. Every one of your other loser friends spent enough time round here watching televised snooker and farting, why didn't he ever pop round eh? I mean, I remember Fat Gary. Creepy Pete and his escaping testicles were a regular feature. But Jeff Goldblum was conspicuous by his absence, Greg!

YES OF COURSE I'M CALLING YOU A FUCKING LIAR!

I'll take whatever tone I want, now listen, *listen* Greg. Greg?

*(JOSIE takes a deep breath.)*

Greg. Where is all my furniture?

No Greg. It wasn't *our* furniture.

In the sense that you didn't choose it or pay for it. In that sense, was not *our* furniture—

I'm upset because there's nothing here! Except for a door stop shaped like a West Highland terrier!

I know you're allergic to dogs, that's not the poin—

You've taken everything! The sofa, the telly, the fridge—

*(As she scans the room itemizing, she looks up for the first time to see the stars twinkling through. She swallows.)*

Gregory. Where's the fucking ROOF gone?!

Greg? Greg? GREG! DO NOT HANG UP ON ME YOU—

*(JOSIE hangs up. She's fuming. She screams in frustration, and slumps on the floor. Right onto the dog doorstop. She pulls it out from under her and throws it across the room. She bursts into tears.)*

**JOSIE.** This isn't happening this isn't happening this isn't happening this isn't—

*(Suddenly a sing-song voice fills the air.)*

**VOICE.** Hell-o!

*(JOSIE starts and looks up.)*

You there!

*(JOSIE looks around, then points to herself, uncertain.)*

Yes you! Grumpy chops lying on the floor and boo-hooing like a big girl! What's the matter? Are you weary? Depressed? Feeling down?

*(JOSIE nods.)*

Can't seem to get those whites white enough or shake those blues away? Need to turn that frown upside down, wash the stains from your existential sheets and start munching at the mango of joy? Do you feel at sixes and sevens? All shook up? Upside down and round the houses? The over-ripe melon that the green-grocer can't shift? Tell me Madam, do you feel like a lonely noodle in the stir fry of life?

*(JOSIE nods vigorously.)*

I thought so! In that case, there's help at hand!

*(There's a knock at the door. JOSIE freezes. There's another knock. JOSIE stands and opens it hesitantly. MARGERY and TERENCE march past her into the flat.)*

**MARGERY.** What gorgeous floors!

**JOSIE.** Sorry, what are you—

**TERENCE.** Hello madam, you must be *Josephine!* Delighted, I'm sure!

*(He shakes* JOSIE's *hand energetically.)*

**MARGERY.** Such light, Terence! Such space!

**TERENCE.** Margery is a keen connoisseur of *ergonomics,* Josephine!

**JOSIE.** I'm sorry but what—I mean, *who*—

**MARGERY.** He is Terence.

**TERENCE.** And she is Margery!

**MARGERY.** For my sins! Ha ha!

**TERENCE.** Ha ha! If you wouldn't mind Madam, say cheese please!

**JOSIE.** What?!

*(*TERENCE *quickly takes her photo.)*

**TERENCE.** Lovely.

**MARGERY.** Your dimensions are *superb!*

**JOSIE.** Get out! Get out of my flat!

*(*MARGERY *and* TERENCE *turn to stare at* JOSIE.)*

**MARGERY.** Not a natural hostess, are you Madam?

**JOSIE.** But—

**TERENCE.** Ah!

**JOSIE.** You—

**TERENCE.** Now then.

*(*TERENCE *and* MARGERY *start bustling about the flat, measuring things and knocking on walls etc etc.* TERENCE *looks up.)*

**TERENCE.** What a tremendous view!

*(*JOSIE *watches them, dumbfounded. She panics for a second, then quickly runs to her hand-bag and rummages in it. She takes out an aerosol can and points it at them like a dangerous weapon.)*

**JOSIE.** You better get out right now! This is mace!

**MARGERY.** No, madam! That's a can of floral scented anti-perspirant for women. It won't have the effect you're looking for at all, I'm afraid.

**TERENCE.** Unless you're planning to *deodorise* us to death! Ha ha!

**MARGERY.** Ha ha!

*(*TERENCE *and* MARGERY *laugh.)*

**MARGERY.** Come now madam, let's not play silly buggers. Put your tongue out please.

*(*JOSIE *hesitates.)*

Chop chop! We haven't got all day, have we? Ha ha.

**TERENCE.** Ha ha!

*(*JOSIE *sticks her tongue out.* TERENCE *takes out a ruler and measures it as* MARGERY *examines it.)*

**MARGERY.** Say aaaah.

**JOSIE.** Aaaah.

**TERENCE.** Just as I thought!

**JOSIE.** Who are you?

**MARGERY.** A category C, would you say Terence?

**TERENCE.** Oh, at least a C, Margery.

**MARGERY.** Can I borrow your telephone? Thank you!

**JOSIE.** I said who are you?!

(MARGERY *takes* JOSIE's *mobile and dials. Her speech on the phone runs over* JOSIE *and* TERENCE's *exchange.*)

**MARGERY.** *Hello! Margery here. Yes that's right. Terence and I are out on an 811. Yes. Yes. Well, the coating of the tongue was not looking happy, Frank. Not happy at all. I think so, don't you? One of the newest models. Yes the Gideon 4000 would be perfect. Smashing. Ok then. See you Frank. Love to Pauline.

**TERENCE.** *We're free-lancers, Madam!

**JOSIE.** Free lance what?

**TERENCE.** Oh, we don't like to go into the *specifics,* Madam.

**JOSIE.** If you don't get out right now, I'm calling the police.

**TERENCE.** If you don't mind me saying Madam, you're coming across as rather *hostile.* Don't you agree Margery?

**MARGERY.** Hmm? Oh yes. Very hostile.

**TERENCE.** Very hostile. Of course that's not unusual.

**MARGERY.** Oh no. Quite par for the course I'd say.

**TERENCE.** Jeff Goldblum was exactly the same.

**JOSIE.** Can everyone please stop talking about Jeff Goldblum!

(MARGERY *and* TERENCE *suck in their breath.*)

**TERENCE.** Madam, let me tell you a story.

**MARGERY.** Oh yes, let's do have a *story* Terence!

**TERENCE.** Margery is *voracious* for narrative, Josephine!

**MARGERY.** Terence tells lovely stories, he can tell you about Orion the hunter, or Taurus, the bull…

**TERENCE.** Or Cassiopeia, Margery! That's a lovely one.

**MARGERY.** Oh yes, tell her about Cassiopeia!

**TERENCE.** Cassiopeia, Josephine, who was turned to stone and hung upside down in the sky by Neptune!

**MARGERY.** We all know that feeling don't we Madam! Upside down! Not quite right! Everything topsy turvey!

**JOSIE.** LOOK! I am really not in the mood for this—this—whatever it is! My ex-fiancé has taken everything I own, my roof is gone, my flat is cold, there's two weirdos standing in my flat and looking at my tongue, I'm tired, and confused, and pissed off. And I haven't had any dinner!

**MARGERY.** Ahhh! The poor child's hungry, Terence!

**TERENCE.** Well why didn't you say!

**MARGERY.** Why didn't you say?

> (TERENCE *pulls out a miniature Cornish pasty from his pocket.*)

**TERENCE.** Mini Cornish pasty for the lady?

**JOSIE.** No. Thank you, I'm—

**MARGERY.** Meat, vegetables, pastry—

**TERENCE.** All the food groups, Josephine! Have a nibble on my pasty. Go on.

**JOSIE.** I don't really like—

**MARGERY / TERENCE.** EAT THE PASTY, JOSEPHINE!

> (*Beat.* JOSIE *shrugs.*)

**JOSIE.** Alright.

> (*She eats the pasty.* MARGERY *and* TERENCE *smile at each other.*)

**JOSIE.** Are you, um—are you two married?

> (TERENCE *and* MARGERY *laugh indulgently.*)

**TERENCE.** Oh no no no no no no no no no no no no no no no no no no no no no no no no no no no no no no NO. Margery is the most incorrigible lesbian you see.

**MARGERY.** And Terence was liberated from carnal desires by an unfortunate incident with a Remington Ladyshave.

**TERENCE.** I'm like a Ken doll down there madam! No, we don't indulge in monogamy ourselves.

**MARGERY.** We merely *facilitate*

**TERENCE.** Enable

**MARGERY.** Plant the seeds

**TERENCE.** And watch them bloom.

> (MARGERY *taps her watch.*)

**MARGERY.** Nearly, Terence.

**TERENCE.** Goodness! Doesn't time *fly* when you're having fun!

**JOSIE.** Nearly what? What's going on?

**TERENCE.** We've taken the liberty of phoning in an order for you.

**MARGERY.** Express delivery! Terence!

> (*They nod at each other.*)

**JOSIE.** *What order? Express delivery of *what*!

**TERENCE / MARGERY.** *Five, four, three, two—

*(They point at the door. There's a knock at the door.)*

**MARGERY.** Right on time!

*(TERENCE gets the door. GIDEON enters. He is carrying a large suitcase and a sleeping mat. He sets both down and does a little bow.)*

**TERENCE.** Gideon, this is Josephine—

**JOSIE.** Josie.

*(GIDEON marches over to JOSIE, throws her over his knee and kisses her like he's Clark Gable. Then stands her up again and returns to his original position.)*

**TERENCE.** Gideon is a top of the range model, Josephine.

**JOSIE.** He, ah, he doesn't say much, does he?

**TERENCE.** Gideon is a man of few words.

**MARGERY.** But *devastating sexuality,* Josephine.

*(JOSIE turns to GIDEON. He smiles at her and does a little jaunty wave.)*

**GIDEON.** Hullo!

**TERENCE.** And now, Margery and I must bid you good-bye.

**MARGERY.** So long, farewell, auf wiedersen

**TERENCE.** Adieu!

**JOSIE.** You're not going—

**TERENCE.** I'm afraid we must. Margery has a pilates class to get to—

**MARGERY.** And Terence is washing his hair tonight! Ha ha!

**TERENCE.** Ha ha!

*(TERENCE and MARGERY laugh. TERENCE explains the joke.)*

**TERENCE.** It's funny, Josephine, because I'm almost entirely bald!

**JOSIE.** Yes, good. Hilarious. But I mean, you're not leaving *him* here. With me?

**MARGERY.** But of course we are!

**TERENCE.** What a question!

**JOSIE.** But I don't want him!

*(MARGERY and TERENCE gasp and MARGERY rushes to put her hands over GIDEON's ears.)*

**TERENCE.** *(Urgent whisper:)* I'm afraid returns aren't permitted until the product has been test-driven for a minimum of *forty eight working hours,* madam.

**JOSIE.** But—

**MARGERY.** We don't make the rules, Josephine. Goodbye.

*(MARGERY and TERENCE exit. JOSIE and GIDEON stand there in silence for a moment or two. Then GIDEON unrolls his sleeping mat and lays it on the floor. Motions for JOSIE to lie down. She hesitates, then does. He lies down next to her.)*

**JOSIE.** You know you can get arthritis from—

**GIDEON.** Shhhhhh.

*(GIDEON points up to the sky.)*

**GIDEON.** Orion.

**JOSIE.** This is weird.

*(He points to a different part of the sky.)*

**GIDEON.** Ursa Major.

**JOSIE.** You're not going to like…kill me and rape my dead body or anything are you?

*(He points again.)*

**GIDEON.** Ursa Minor.

**JOSIE.** You probably wouldn't say if you were, would you? I mean.

*(He points again.)*

**GIDEON.** Andromeda.

**JOSIE.** That would be silly.

*(He points again.)*

**GIDEON.** Cassiopeia.

**JOSIE.** I'm going to shut up now.

*(A pause.)*

**JOSIE.** Do you, ah…do you…do you…want some tea?

*(GIDEON shakes his head. Points.)*

**GIDEON.** Cassiopeia.

**JOSIE.** Some ah…soup?

*(GIDEON shakes his head again. Points.)*

**GIDEON.** Cassiopeia.

**JOSIE.** That's good. Cos I don't have any soup. I don't know why I just offered you soup when I don't have any that was…

*(GIDEON stands up.)*

…silly where are you going?

*(JOSIE stands up too and starts to follow him.)*

*(GIDEON holds up a finger: 'wait.' JOSIE stops. GIDEON crosses to the suitcase on the other side of the room, carries it to centre-stage, sets it down. Very methodically, he snaps the locks and opens it. It's empty…)*

*(Except for: one red helium balloon. With great ceremony, he holds it by the string, smiles and holds it out to her.)*

*(She takes it. Stares at it. A beat. Then she smiles.)*

*(They look at each other for a long time.)*

*(Then* JOSIE *lets go of the balloon.)*

*(It floats up to the stars.)*

*(Blackout.)*

*("Life" by Sly and the Family Stone plays very loudly indeed.)*

## *End of Play*

# THE RUMOR
## by Dan Kois

## APHY

⌐⌐  s was the founding editor of *New York* magazine's arts and culture blog, *Vulture*. He has written for *New York*, *The New York Times*, *The Washington Post*, *Slate*, and other newspapers and magazines. He lives in the Washington, D.C. area with his wife and children. He is right-handed.

His first book, part of the *33 1/3* series, is about Hawaiian singer Israel Kamakawiwo'ole and will be published in 2009.

## ACKNOWLEDGMENTS

*The Rumor* was originally produced by The 24 Hour Company at The Atlantic Theater in New York City on June 3, 2002. It directed by Stu Zicherman with the following cast:

| | |
|---|---|
| PR FLACK | Danita Winfield |
| REPORTER 1 | Tor Ekeland |
| REPORTER 2 | Brice Gaillard |
| CHUCK BONNER | Garrett Savage |
| CHRIS TINGLEY | Sean Williams |
| LARRY WAKEFIELD | Bradford Olson |

# CAST OF CHARACTERS

PR FLACK
TWO REPORTERS (playing multiple roles)
CHUCK BONNER
CHRIS TINGLEY
LARRY WAKEFIELD

## PRODUCTION NOTES

A note on the type: A slash / in a line marks the point of interruption for the next line. For instance, in the following exchange:

**R2.** The guy got the game-winning RBI, he can't spare ten minutes / for us?

**FLACK.** He's with ESPN.

The cue for the Flack's line "He's with ESPN" is Reporter 2 saying the word "minutes."

Occasionally, lines will continue through an interruption. For instance, in the following exchange:

**R1.** Your former teammate, Eric Davis / made headlines

**TINGLEY.** Ah, Eric.

**R1.** a few seasons ago by saying that he wouldn't share a glove...

The cue for Tingley's line "Ah, Eric" is Reporter 1 saying the word "Davis." Reporter 1 continues through her next line *without pause.*

# THE RUMOR

*Lights up on a table with three microphones. Reporters are arrayed before the table, waiting for the press conference to begin. A PR FLACK is briefing them.*

**FLACK.** We'll have Larry Wakefield, Chris Tingley, and Chuck Bonner out to talk about the game in a moment. FYI, Boston lost tonight so the Yanks are a half-game out.

**R1.** What about Castillo?

**FLACK.** He's with ESPN.

**R1.** Fuckin' ESPN.

**R2.** The guy got the game-winning RBI, he can't spare ten minutes / for us?

**FLACK.** He's with ESPN.

**R1.** Fuckin' ESPN.

**R2.** Will Bonner be addressing Tony's column in the *Post?*

**FLACK.** I can't speak to that, Linda.

**R2.** So, yeah?

*(WAKEFIELD, TINGLEY, and BONNER enter and sit at the table. They have all recently showered and still have wet hair. WAKEFIELD wears a Yankees hat and a warm-up jacket. TINGLEY wears a muscle shirt with cut-off sleeves and is chewing gum. BONNER has a towel hung around his neck.)*

**R1.** Nice throwin' today, Chuck!

**BONNER.** Thanks.

**R1.** Love that sinker to / Mendoza.

**R2.** Chris, were you looking fastball on the homer?

**TINGLEY.** Yeah.

**FLACK.** Chuck has a prepared statement to read.

*(Clamor.)*

Chuck has a prepared statement and then they'll all take questions.

**BONNER.** Thank you.

*(Reads from a prepared statement:)*

"We live in a society where baseball players are looked up to as heroes. Right or wrong, I know that as a player for the greatest team in the world, my life a public one. But I try to keep my private life as private as possible. However, recent rumors, including an irresponsible column in yesterday's *New York Post*, force me to respond.

I know that I live in America, the greatest country in the world, and that part of that greatness is freedom of the press. But I resent these rumors and I resent the fact that I have been forced to dignify them with a response. So I will just say it, right here, right now, so that there can be no confusion: I am not ambidextrous."

    *(Clamor.)*

**FLACK.** Prepared statement, guys, then questions.

**BONNER.** "I am a right-handed pitcher. I pitch with my right hand. I cannot, nor do I want to, throw with my left hand. I only pitch with my right hand. Thank you."

**FLACK.** Questions?

    *(Clamor.)*

Gary.

**R1.** Chuck, Tony Franklin's *Post* column didn't mention any names at all.

**BONNER.** Right.

**R1.** It just said, I'll quote here: "There's a persistent rumor around town that one Yankees star who spends a lot of time throwing the ball with his right hand is actually ambidextrous and has started to think about declaring his manual orientation." Why do you think the column's about you?

**BONNER.** I don't know who the column's about. You'll have to ask Tony Franklin that.

**R1.** Sorry, I'll rephrase. Do Yankees fans think the column is about you?

**BONNER.** I can't control what people think. That's obvious. And I can't convince people what to think. I can only say what I know and what the truth is and that's I'm right-handed and I throw with my right hand. That's it. End of story.

    *(Clamor.)*

**FLACK.** Yes, Anne.

**R2.** Coach, is there an ambidextrous player on the Yankees?

**WAKEFIELD.** I don't know. Not that it's anyone's business, but I don't know. I never walked in on anyone throwing with both hands, if that's what you mean.

    *(Clamor.)*

**FLACK.** Barry?

**R1.** Coach, can you explain the comments you made to *Esquire* magazine last month?

**WAKEFIELD.** Whaddya mean, explain?

**R1.** Well, / I mean—

**WAKEFIELD.** What's to explain?

**R1.** Coach—

**WAKEFIELD.** Next question.

(Clamor.)

**FLACK.** Okay—

**WAKEFIELD.** "Explain." Are the majors are ready for an openly ambidextrous player? I said sure. What's to explain?

**R1.** Do you still feel that way, after all the attention / this issue has gotten?

**WAKEFIELD.** Yeah, sure I do. We're all big boys here.

**FLACK.** Latonya?

**R2.** Chris, how do *you* feel? Are the majors ready for a player who openly has the ability to throw with both hands?

**TINGLEY.** In this day and age it would be irrelevant. If the guy is doing his job on the field, you know, I don't think there would be any problem at all.

**BONNER.** I agree.

**TINGLEY.** There's practical considerations, though.

**BONNER.** Yeah.

**TINGLEY.** Like, what hand does he wear his glove on?

**BONNER.** Sure, yeah.

(Clamor.)

**FLACK.** Bobby?

**R1.** Nice game today, Chris.

**TINGLEY.** Thanks, Bobby.

**R1.** Your former teammate, Eric Davis / made headlines

**TINGLEY.** Ah, Eric.

**R1.** a few seasons ago by saying that he wouldn't share a glove with an ambidextrous teammate.

**TINGLEY.** I remember.

**R1.** He said, I'm paraphrasing here, but he said, "I have no problem with switch-hitters, but I don't want someone on my team going around throwing with both hands."

**TINGLEY.** Right.

**R1.** "That's just plain weird," he said.

**TINGLEY.** Right.

**R1.** Do you think his feelings are shared by many big leaguers?

**TINGLEY.** No.

**BONNER.** No.

**TINGLEY.** Nuh-uh, it's just, ballplayers are never / gonna…

**BONNER.** We're not the most open-minded / people on earth…

**TINGLEY.** Right, but we're still / fairly…

**BONNER.** We're not going to, y'know, walk into an ambidextrous bar and start, like—

**TINGLEY.** — playing darts.

**BONNER.** With both hands.

**TINGLEY.** No.

**WAKEFIELD.** But on the whole, I think major leaguers are pretty accepting.

**TINGLEY.** Eric, I love Eric, but he's sort of from the old school, you know.

**BONNER.** *(Nodding:)* Old / school.

**WAKEFIELD.** Old school.

    *(Clamor.)*

**FLACK.** Yeah, Alia.

**R2.** Coach, what kind of player should be that trailblazer? The Jackie Robinson of ambidexterity?

**TINGLEY.** Good question. / Good question.

**BONNER.** Good question.

**WAKEFIELD.** Well—it shouldn't matter—but it'd be best if he's a real superstar, like Jackie was.

**TINGLEY.** That's why there's rumors about Chuck, you know. When you're getting near 300 wins, that's a big deal, and if he was ambidextrous, which he's not, but if he were, he'd be a real ambassador.

**BONNER.** Sure.

**WAKEFIELD.** Beyond that, I don't know. Whoever he is—like Jackie— whoever he is, he shouldn't be such a, a, in-your-face ambidextrous guy. He should be proud, but he should have that—dignity.

**BONNER.** It's best if he's not flamboyantly ambidextrous.

**TINGLEY.** Using both hands all the time in public, right.

    *(Clamor.)*

**FLACK.** Lance?

**R1.** Fellas, even the most conservative estimates from scientists suggest that two to four percent of Americans are ambidextrous. So it would seem like at least 15 / to 30 major leaguers…

**BONNER.** That's high. That's just math.

**WAKEFIELD.** Lance, this isn't the general population, you know? This is baseball. Single-handedness is very important, it's a really prominent part of the culture of baseball, you know, the locker room and all.

**R1.** But still, there must be at least one or two / who are in the closet.

**BONNER.** Sure. / Sure.

**TINGLEY.** Sure. We've played with guys, with guys who, you know, who weren't *out* out but who it was a known secret on the team, you know?

**R1.** And no one had any—

**BONNER.** No. No problem.

　　　　*(Tiny pause.)*

**R1.** Was this on the Dodgers?

**BONNER.** I'm not, no, I'm not / identi—

**R1.** Was it—

**WAKEFIELD.** That's fruitless, Lance. Next question. That young lady over there has been waving her hands for a while.

**FLACK.** Yes, Miss…

**R2.** Lucinda Martin, *Both Hands Magazine.*

**BONNER.** Oh, Christ.

**R2.** Mr. Bonner, do you have a problem with ambidextrous people?

**BONNER.** No, I do not.

**R2.** Does this so-called rumor threaten your handhood? Do you see something wrong / with ambidexterity?

**BONNER.** No.

**WAKEFIELD.** Can someone—

**R2.** Do you feel—

**FLACK.** Miss, please let Mr. Bonner answer your questions.

**R2.** Sure, fine.

**BONNER.** I have no problem whatsoever with ambidextrous people. Okay? I, I'm not one, but I, like I said before, I have played with them before, and I have friends, and I'm just saying—it's not me. I'll tell Yankees fans right now, the greatest fans in the world, ambidextrous people are people just like you and me.

**R2.** Mr. Bonner, I'm ambidextrous.

**BONNER.** That's great.

**R2.** Like many ambidextrous people, my favorite baseball player is Chuck Bonner. You actually have quite a fan base among the ambi community. Would you like to speculate on why this is?

**BONNER.** *(Pained:)* No, that's great. I'm always grateful for my fans, no matter who they are or how many of their hands they can use with equal ability.

**R2.** What would you say if I told you we had pictures—

**FLACK.** Okay, / that's enough.

**R2.** Pictures of you throwing with your left hand in high school?

**TINGLEY.** Someone shut her the fuck up!

**R2.** What would you say?

**BONNER.** I'd say you were a liar. You can do anything with photos these days.

**R2.** But these pictures—

**R1.** Shut up! Let the rest of us go!

**TINGLEY.** Those pictures are bullshit, just for the record.

**R2.** You can't lie to yourself forever, Bonner!

**FLACK.** *(Very firm:)* That is absolutely enough, Miss Martin. If you cannot speak civilly to these players I will have you removed. Next question, right here in the front.

**R1.** Chuck, can you prove you're not ambidextrous?

**WAKEFIELD.** Oh, for Chrissakes—

**R1.** Our readers want to know if a major New York figure is hiding a newsworthy fact about himself!

**TINGLEY.** This is not / *newsworthy.*

**BONNER.** Carter, ask anyone who knows me. Ask anyone who—

**R1.** Can you prove it?

**BONNER.** Fine. Fuck. Fine.

> *(*BONNER *tromps out into the reporter pool.)*

Gimme your— gimme your notebook.

**TINGLEY.** Chuck—

**BONNER.** Gimme your fucking notebook. And your pen. Here. I'm writing with my left hand. Look at this!

> *(He holds the notebook up. In extremely childish, sloppy lettering: FUCK YOU.)*

Is that proof enough? Is that proof enough? How about this?

> *(He throws the notebook at* REPORTER 2 *with his left hand, missing by a mile. His throwing motion is exaggeratedly awkward, almost girlish. He is furious, near tears.)*

**TINGLEY.** Chuck!

**BONNER.** How about that? Did you get your pictures? Did you get all that? Why does everyone think I'm hiding something, that I'm—why? No, tell me. Why? Do you ask Greg Maddux if he's ambidextrous? Do you ask Randy Johnson? Well, do you?

**TINGLEY.** *(Softly:)* No.

**BONNER.** No! What if I *was* an ambidextrous man? What if I *was?* How would this fucking witch-hunt make me feel? What kind of message does that send to the world?

**TINGLEY.** Chuck, honey…

*(TINGLEY takes BONNER's hand and strokes it. BONNER is crying. TINGLEY gently kisses BONNER's forehead.)*

**BONNER.** I'm so tired, Chris.

**TINGLEY.** I know.

**BONNER.** What if I was? What if I was tired of keeping secrets?

*(Pause.)*

**TINGLEY.** Then you'd have to stop keeping them.

**R1.** What are you saying, Chuck?

**TINGLEY.** *(To the reporter:)* Shut up.

**BONNER.** *(Ignoring the reporter:)* What if I was tired?

*(Pause.)*

**R2.** Chris? Is this something you and your husband have discussed?

*(Pause. WAKEFIELD makes a cut-off gesture to the FLACK.)*

**FLACK.** Okay, this press conference is over—

**BONNER.** No.

**TINGLEY.** Chuck?

**BONNER.** *No.*

*(BONNER looks over at WAKEFIELD, who nods solemnly. BONNER faces the crowd.)*

I have something I would like to say.

*(Blackout.)*

## End of Play

# RECESS
## (WHERE IS THE TERRORISM IN US?)
## by Richard LaGravenese

Richard LaGravenese was born and raised in Brooklyn, New York. He attended Emerson College and NYU's Experimental Theatre Wing at the Tisch School of the Arts.

He wrote (and sold) his first piece of writing for the Off Broadway musical revue, *A My Name is Alice* directed by Joan Michlin Silver. His sketch material for a comedy duo act led to an offer by former Saturday Night Live writer Neil Levy, to co-write the script for the 1989 release, *Rude Awakening*.

Mr. LaGravenese began his solo screenwriting career with his original screenplay *The Fisher King*, directed by Terry Gilliam. The film went on to earn five Academy Award nominations, including Best Screenplay, winning Best Supporting Actress for Mercedes Ruehl. His subsequent screenwriting credits include: *The Ref*, (directed by Ted Demme), *A Little Princess* (directed by Alfonso Cuaron), *Unstrung Heroes* (directed by Diane Keaton), *The Bridges of Madison County* (directed by Clint Eastwood), *The Mirror Has Two Faces* (directed by Barbra Streisand), *The Horse Whisperer* (directed by Robert Redford), and *Beloved* (directed by Jonathon Demme).

Mr. LaGravenese directed his original screenplay for the critically acclaimed *Living Out Loud* starring Danny DeVito, Holly Hunter and Queen Latifah. He joined other directors for the omnibus *Paris J'taime* with stars Fanny Ardent and Bob Hoskins.

In 2007, Mr. LaGravenese wrote and directed two film releases: *Freedom Writers*, starring Hilary Swank and Patrick Dempsey (the screenplay was awarded the Humanitas Prize); *P.S. I Love You*, with Hilary Swank, Kathy Bates, Gerard Butler, Lisa Kudrow, Harry Connick Jr., Gina Gershon and Jeffrey Dean Morgan.

Mr. LaGravenese co-directed and co-produced (with the late Ted Demme), a three-part documentary for IFC entitled *A Decade Under the Influence*, which explores the breakthrough films and filmmakers of the 1970s. The film won the National Board of Review William K. Everson Award for film history and earned an Emmy nomination for best documentary.

## ACKNOWLEDGMENTS

*Recess* was originally produced by The 24 Hour Company at The Minetta Lane Theater in New York City on September 24, 2001. It was directed by Anna Strasberg and featured the following cast:

KYRA .................................................................. Kyra Sedgwick
JULIANNE .......................................................... Julianne Moore
CATHERINE ...................................................... Catherine Kellner

## CAST OF CHARACTERS

KYRA, an envious, power-mad dictator.

JULIANNE, a passive aggressive power intent on survival.

CATHERINE, a well intentioned newcomer who turns defiant.

## PRODUCTION NOTE

Swiftly paced, at times.

# RECESS

*Open on:* KYRA *and* JULIANNE *are fifth grade N.Y. private school teachers, sitting on the grass, watching over their students during recess…as they talk…*

**KYRA.** After twelve years of teaching fifth grade I've come to realize that deep down, I don't really like children.

**JULIANNE.** I know. *(Beat, admits:)* I don't like girls.

**KYRA.** Oh girls are terrifying.

**JULIANNE.** They're so cruel. Mean. Deliberately. I watch it. They know exactly what to say to inflict pain. I watched them torture this girl, who's a little overweight…in Mrs. Cantor's class—I was shocked. The things they said.

**KYRA.** And they enjoy it.

**JULIANNE.** And they enjoy it. I was shocked.

**KYRA.** There's nothing you can do.

**JULIANNE.** No, there's nothing. I just stood and watched with my mouth open.

**KYRA.** Kids have to learn to deal with that kind of person. There are people in the world who enjoy being cruel and they have to learn to deal with it… We did.

**JULIANNE.** I never understood "enjoying being cruel."

**KYRA.** No, me neither.

*(KYRA looks to the field and yells [at the audience]:)*

BILLY! BILLY MILLER!…

*(Gets his attention:)*

This is your first warning.

*(She holds up one finger.)*

He's a monster. I can't wait until he goes to the Upper school. If he lasts that long. You can tell by his reading and math skills—he'll never be more than a C student. He doesn't really belong here.

**JULIANNE.** I remember teaching second grade knowing immediately who would make it and who wouldn't.

**KYRA.** How long did you teach second grade?

**JULIANNE.** One year. My first year.

**KYRA.** One year? *(Disturbed:)* And then you went straight to fifth?

**JULIANNE.** Hmmm-mmm

**KYRA.** *(Hiding her irritation:)* Well.

*(Beat. They look out to the field.)*

**JULIANNE.** Should we give them their juice?

**KYRA.** *(Quickly:)* No— *(Shifts quickly:)* Usually you can't just move that quickly to the higher grades.

**JULIANNE.** How long did it take you?

**KYRA.** Four years... *(Shifts quickly, disturbed:)* I thought you were in second grade much longer.

**JULIANNE.** No.

*(Beat. JULIANNE looks out to the field. KYRA re-groups.)*

**KYRA.** I remember now, when you were hired. That was a very bad period.

**JULIANNE.** What do you mean?

**KYRA.** *(Looking out:)* Well it was very difficult to get anyone qualified. There simply weren't any qualified teachers applying.

*(Beat. Kyra's dart lands. JULIANNE feels stung but doesn't know how to take it. But she's clearly intimidated by KYRA...cautious.)*

**JULIANNE.** *(Timidly:)* Well...I taught at public school for three years.

**KYRA.** *(Tosses off:)* It's not the same... *(Yells to field:)* BILLY!... Warning number Two.

*(She holds up two fingers.)*

*(JULIANNE doesn't want any trouble. She looks to the field, refers to a third teacher, CATHERINE, who is in the field with her class.)*

**JULIANNE.** Have you gotten to know the replacement for Mrs. Yullip? I can't stand her. She's just trying too hard to be one of the gang—don't you think?

**KYRA.** Young.

**JULIANNE.** My God. I don't even think she has any experience.

**KYRA.** With that ass, she doesn't need it.

**JULIANNE.** *(Laughs.)* Stop.

**KYRA.** She must be blowing the headmaster.

**JULIANNE.** *(Laughs.)* Stop.

**KYRA.** It's not like he doesn't try.

**JULIANNE.** You too? I'm uncomfortable around him. I'd avoid him every chance I got.

**KYRA.** He's harmless. He tried—brushed by my ass in the hallway with his hand. I ignored it. It went away.

**JULIANNE.** Well, I couldn't ignore it. He asked me out.

*(KYRA is caught off guard by this. JULIANNE knows she's hit her target, "innocently.")*

**KYRA.** On a date?

**JULIANNE.** Yes. My first year. To dinner and a show.

**KYRA.** *(Getting pissed:)* What show?

**JULIANNE.** Oh God, what was it… Some awful musical based on *The House of Mirth*… I think… I don't even remember. I wanted to be polite… I was new. But it was so awkward when he took me home. I mean, we kissed but very politely.

**KYRA.** And that was it?

**JULIANNE.** He asked several times after. I went to a few things but then I met Steve and getting married saved me. I was able to say no and not alienate him. But still he likes to kiss me on the cheek during orientation.

**KYRA.** *(Looking right at JULIANNE:)* Pig.

**JULIANNE.** *(Looking out:)* Really.

> *(CATHERINE comes quickly down the aisle—"from the field"—up on stage and sits beside the two teachers who welcome her.)*

**CATHERINE.** HI!

**JULIANNE.** Hi. You're great out there!

**KYRA.** Hi. Come sit!

**CATHERINE.** Oh, I can't run anymore. They never stop. I haven't played dodge ball in a hundred years.

**KYRA.** I won't let my class play it. I think it's too violent.

**CATHERINE.** Oh… Well, I don't know… They enjoy it. Gets all their frustrations out. They don't throw it that hard.

**JULIANNE.** The boys do. The boys really want to hurt you.

**KYRA.** *(To CATHERINE:)* You don't want an injury your first year. You should tell them to stop.

**CATHERINE.** I don't know—my girls are tough—they can take care of themselves.

> *(Beat. All three look out to the field. Then:)*

**KYRA.** *(Faux sympathy:)* So, how are you doing? Are you managing? Being a replacement?

**CATHERINE.** It's great. The faculty is really nice. I still don't everyone by name yet…

**KYRA.** Don't worry. The faculty changes so often, there's no point in remembering names. I'm one of the few teachers that's been here longer than ten years.

**CATHERINE.** *(Impressed:)* You've been here ten years?

**KYRA / JULIANNE.** Twelve.

**CATHERINE.** Wow.

**JULIANNE.** I've been here seven.

**CATHERINE.** That's great. Maybe I should talk to both of you then. I was thinking of asking the headmaster to give us a little more leeway on the reading list. I mean, these books they give the kids— They're so awful.

**JULIANNE.** Which ones?

**CATHERINE.** *(Thinks:)* Oh, hmm… OH, like *The Rainbow Bag.*

**JULIANNE.** That actually won a Newberry Award.

**CATHERINE.** Like 35 years ago. Kids today are much more sophisticated, don't you think? The writing is so sophomoric.

**JULIANNE.** My class loves it.

**CATHERINE.** It doesn't interest mine.

**KYRA.** *(Friendly, "helpful":)* Maybe it's the way you teach it.

> *(Beat. CATHERINE can sense KYRA's hostility and it doesn't faze her.)*

**CATHERINE.** *(Tries to be nice:)* Maybe. I know there are better books. Books the kids can relate to.

**KYRA.** Well, that's the problem I think—teachers today want to cater to their needs. They're always trying to relate to them. I mean, our teachers didn't care about relating to us. We had to stretch ourselves. This new way of teaching is ruining our children. It breaks my heart.

**CATHERINE.** *(Getting pissed:)* What new way of teaching?

**JULIANNE.** *(Calming things:)* Have you ever read the *Oz* books? They're lovely. Not just the first one—the whole collection. I wish we could let the kids read those.

**KYRA.** *(Dismissive:)* That's a third and fourth reading level. It's too easy for fifth graders.

**JULIANNE.** My class loves them.

**KYRA.** *(Looking out:)* Well, YOUR class would.

> *(Beat. JULIANNE feels beaten down again. CATHERINE tries another tactic.)*

**CATHERINE.** Maybe I'll just put together a mock list and we can all give our suggestions and if we all agree, we'll submit it to the headmaster.

**KYRA.** No.

**CATHERINE.** What?

**KYRA.** No. And I don't mean to dampen your enthusiasm. I think it's wonderful you want to try to do the best you can given the circumstances. But I have seniority at the fifth level and I don't want the reading list changed so I don't want you to go out of your way to put together a whole list or anything. But what I will do, if you like, if you need ANY help at all with your lesson plans or your approach to the books, I would be more than willing to help. I really think if you put a little more effort in what's proven effective before you arrived, you might get some wonderful results in time.

*(Beat.* JULIANNE *sinks a little, in between the two.* CATHERINE *takes this in her stride, nodding.)*

**CATHERINE.** OK… Well, how about I make the list anyway, submit it to the headmaster and you can just lick my ass.

*(Beat. Confronted,* KYRA *is at a loss for words.* JULIANNE *senses a shift in power…and keeps silent.)*

*(Suddenly,* KYRA *stands, turning to the field, screaming:)*

**KYRA.** *(Enraged:)* BILLY MILLER… GET OVER HERE… RIGHT NOW…

*(Two beats until he arrives—to* BILLY:*)*

That was your third warning! I don't want to hear any excuses. I am sending a note to your parents and you will sit with Mr. Shelstein in the admissions office during recess for the rest of the week.

*(*CATHERINE *and* JULIANNE *grow uncomfortable at her fury:)*

Don't tell me you don't know what you did? I will not have that kind of behavior! That kind of behavior is unacceptable! Especially for a C student. Do you know you're lucky to even be here!? Now, come with me!!

*(She looks to the teachers then exits.)*

**JULIANNE.** Oh, I'm so glad you said that. I can't stand her.

**CATHERINE.** My God. Should she talk to the kids like that?

**JULIANNE.** Are you married?

**CATHERINE.** Yeah.

**JULIANNE.** Any children?

**CATHERINE.** We're trying. You?

**JULIANNE.** I have a girl. Two.

**CATHERINE.** Oooh, a little girl. I want a little girl.

**JULIANNE.** Girls are great. Much better than boys.

*End of Play*

# MARS HAS NEVER BEEN THIS CLOSE

## by Warren Leight

## BIOGRAPHY

Warren Leight's *Side Man* won the 1999 Tony Award for Best Play. His other plays include *No Foreigners Beyond This Point* (Baltimore Center Stage premiere); *James and Annie* (Ensemble Theatre of Cincinnati premiere); *Glimmer, Glimmer and Shine* (ATCA Nomination); *Mayor, the Musical* (Drama Desk Nomination); *Fame Takes a Holiday* (co-written); *Stray Cats;* and *The Loop*. Recent publications: *Dark No Sugar*, a collection of one acts; *Leading Women: Plays for Actresses II;* DPS's *Outstanding Men's Monologues 2001-2002;* Ensemble Studio Theatre's Marathon 2000 collection; and *Dramatics* magazine. Screenplays include *The Night We Never Met* (starring Matthew Broderick and Annabella Sciorra), which he also directed. He was formerly showrunner on *Law & Order: Criminal Intent* and is currently showrunner on HBO's *In Treatment;* and member of the Dramatists Guild Council.

## ACKNOWLEDGMENTS

*Mars Has Never Been This Close* was originally produced by The 24 Hour Company at The American Airlines Theatre in New York City on September 15, 2003. It was directed by Annie Dorsen with the following cast:

| | |
|---|---|
| GREGORY | Andre Royo |
| SAM | Liev Schreiber |
| MARK | Griffin Dunne |
| EARL | Giancarlo Esposito |
| CHRIS | Alan Cumming |

## CAST OF CHARACTERS

GREGORY
SAM
MARK
EARL
CHRIS

# Mars Has Never Been This Close

*A wedding party at the Greenwich Country Club, night. Downstage, at a table, drinking by himself, sits* CHRIS. *Upstage, on one side of the deck, overlooking the bay,* SAM *looks up at the sky. Reflective.* GREGORY *comes up to him.*

**GREGORY.** Sir—

**SAM.** You know Gregory, they say Mars hasn't been this close to the Earth in millions of years.

**GREGORY.** Yes, sir. I just wanted to let you know we are beginning to serve dinner.

**SAM.** Thanks, I'll…just be a minute.

*(SAM takes out a cell phone, and dials someone.)*

*(MARK and* DR. EARL CLEMENS, *on the other side of the deck.* MARK *has a drink in one hand, a small envelope in the other. He reads the small card that came from the small envelope.)*

**MARK.** Table Fourteen?

**EARL.** Let's don't.

**MARK.** It's Siberia.

**EARL.** Let's not.

**MARK.** Table fourteen? They…put us in the ghetto. You literally save her mother's life, and they put us—

**EARL.** Mark let's just try to have a good time.

**MARK.** Do you think either of us would be allowed into this club, if it weren't a wedding.

**EARL.** We'd have no desire to be here if it weren't Mary's wedding.

*(MARK sees GREGORY crossing past.)*

**MARK.** Oh look, another person of color. How did that happen?

*(Waves.)*

**EARL.** Mark—

*(GREGORY comes over.)*

**GREGORY.** Can I help you find your table sir.

*(MARK gives EARL a "what I tell you look?")*

**MARK.** We're at fourteen.

**GREGORY.** *(Underwhelmed:)* Fourteen? It's down those stairs.

**MARK.** Thank you.

**GREGORY.** *(He points.)* With that other…gentleman.

**MARK.** Thank you, oh I'll, uh…need a refill.

**GREGORY.** Yes sir. Right away.

(EARL *reacts to Mark's drinking.*)

**MARK.** *(To* EARL:*)* What? It's a Wasp wedding. When in Rye, drink it.

(*Before he can answer,* MARK *goes to the table, where* CHRIS, *also quite smashed, knocks back his drink.*)

Ahoy. Fellow outcast.

**CHRIS.** I prefer to think of myself as aloof.

**MARK.** Very Garbo.

**EARL.** *(Sits next to* MARK.*)* Garbo? You're dating yourself.

**MARK.** Somebody has to.

**EARL.** Not if this keeps up.

**CHRIS.** Okayyy. So—are you two lovebirds friends of the bride, or the groom.

**MARK.** Neither.

**EARL.** I'm Dr. Clemens, Earl, and—

**CHRIS.** Oh yes, the one who saved Mary's mother.

**EARL.** I didn't really—

**MARK.** He did.

**CHRIS.** *(To* MARK:*)* An oncologist boyfriend. Your mother must be very proud.

**MARK.** I haven't had the heart to tell her about us yet. *(Whispers:)* He's not Jewish.

**CHRIS.** You saved her mother's life, and they seat you here. God, these people.

**MARK.** *(To* EARL:*)* I didn't bring it up—

**CHRIS.** It's all so…Connecticut Nazi. I think the only reason they don't make us wear yellow stars is it would clash with all the mint green pants…

(*Off Earl's lack of amusement:*)

Doctor, is something wrong?

**EARL.** I just think it's a little facile to judge people on the basis of superficial choices. Or long held traditions, or—

**CHRIS.** Well, there goes my whole way of life.

(MARK *and* CHRIS *clink glasses.*)

**SAM.** *(Joining:)* Is this Table Fourteen.

**MARK.** Is the Pope gay?

(SAM, *not getting it, but laughing along.*)

**SAM.** I'm Sam. I guess we're the bachelor table tonight. Friends of the…?

**MARK.** —bride—ish. I'm Mark. This is Earl. The bride's brother. Just kidding.

**CHRIS.** I dated the groom. Not kidding.

*(Off of everyone's look:)*

At Buckley.

**MARK.** Buckley. Oh, that doesn't count, that's called youthful experimentation.

**CHRIS.** We kept seeing each other, once in a while, up until a few months ago. He's insatiable.

**SAM.** *(Again, not getting it, but laughing:)* This is a funny table. You guys are funny.

**MARK.** *(To SAM:)* And what planet do you come from?

**SAM.** Finance, like everyone else.

**MARK.** What else is there, really?

**GREGORY.** Gentlemen. Your drinks.

**CHRIS.** Keep them coming. *(To the others:)* I have to make a toast to the happy couple.

**GREGORY.** Yes sir. And will you be having the steak, or the salmon.

**EARL.** Which do you recommend?

**GREGORY.** They're both very good, sir.

**MARK.** There's a surprise.

**CHRIS.** Do you know where the salmon comes from?

**GREGORY.** I imagine the ocean, sir.

**CHRIS.** *(Off the others' looks:)* It actually matters. You know what they do to salmon these days. They ask the farmer what color he wants it to be, they inject it with dyes, then they let them swim around in tanks filled with their own feces, while they feed them food laced with PCBs.

**SAM.** I'll have the salmon.

**EARL.** Sounds good.

**MARK.** Me too.

**CHRIS.** Make it four. And another one of these.

**MARK.** Two.

**GREGORY.** Very good gentlemen. Four salmons.

**MARK.** Poor guy must go crazy working here.

**SAM.** Gregory's father worked at the club for years. He's worked his way up from ball boy.

**CHRIS.** What a success story.

**EARL.** *(Trying to change the subject, to SAM:)* Wasn't the bride just absolutely stunning?

**SAM.** Totally.

**CHRIS.** She's not my type.

**MARK.** Sounds like she's not the groom's type either.

**EARL.** Her mother tells me they are very happy.

**MARK.** Of course, the wedding *was* postponed from the spring.

　　　*(He looks at* CHRIS.*)*

**SAM.** Oh that—Mary got upset, when she found his porno collection.

**CHRIS.** She what?

**SAM.** He tried to tell her it was no big deal. I mean, all guys have some, right. But I think she was upset…about the specifics.

**MARK.** Backdoor?

**SAM.** Actually

　　　*(Leans in.)*

"Ghetto Booty, Part Two…"

**CHRIS.** Part Two?

**MARK.** You should never get the sequels, they only make them for the money.

**SAM.** *(Not getting any of this:)* Mary was shaken up, but my wife finally told her the best thing was just to ignore it.

**CHRIS.** Your wife?

**SAM.** *(Again, not getting it:)* She couldn't make it.

**MARK.** That's his story, and he's sticking to it.

**SAM.** She's in the city. Chemo. Didn't feel up to traveling.

**EARL.** *(To* MARK:*)* Open mouth, take out Prada.

**MARK.** I'm sorry, I didn't know.

**SAM.** It's all right. She's going to be fine.

**EARL.** I hope so.

**SAM.** She will. She's a great gal. I called her from the deck, told her about Mars. How close it is. How it's a sign she can fight this thing.

**EARL.** Where is she getting her—

**MARK.** You're off-duty Earl, remember?

　　　*(*GREGORY *comes by, with drinks for* CHRIS, SAM, *and* MARK.*)*

Gregory, my good man.

**CHRIS.** You might as well bring me another, with the salmon.

**MARK.** Me too.

　　　*(*EARL *signals* GREGORY *"no,"* GREGORY *is unsure of what to do.)*

**EARL.** Mark—it's a long drive.

**MARK.** For fuck sake, Earl, don't be such a fun cop. *(To* GREGORY:*)* Gregory—what are you waiting for?

*(Pulls out a five dollar bill.)*

Hup hup.

**GREGORY.** Yes sir.

*(He goes.* MARK *looks at* EARL, *he's desperate for a reaction.* EARL *almost loses it.)*

**EARL.** That…was uncalled for.

**MARK.** "Uncalled for"? That's it? That's all you have to say. What is wrong with you Earl. Don't you get it? You're never going to be one of them. You can save Mary's mother, or maybe Sam's wife. It won't help. No matter how hard you work, no matter how hard you try to be perfect, as far as this world is concerned, the most you are ever going to be is the hired help.

**EARL.** *(Gets up, angry…but restrains himself.)* I'm going to…get some air.

*(He walks out.)*

**MARK.** *(To* SAM *and* CHRIS:*)* Couple stuff. He'll be back.

**SAM.** You…you shouldn't take people for granted. You just…

*(*SAM *walks out, in Earl's direction.)*

**MARK.** You're right *(To* CHRIS:*)* Now what?

*(CHRIS *gets a big, kind of scary smile. He clinks a fork against his glass, slowly rises to his feet.)*

**CHRIS.** I'd like, to propose a toast.

*(Lights out.)*

*End of Play*

# THAT OTHER PERSON
## by David Lindsay-Abaire

## BIOGRAPHY

David Lindsay-Abaire was most recently awarded the 2008 Ed Kleban Award as America's most promising musical theatre lyricist. Prior to that, he received the 2007 Pulitzer Prize for Drama for his play *Rabbit Hole*, which premiered on Broadway at MTC's Biltmore Theatre. *Rabbit Hole* also received five Tony Award nominations, including Best Play, and the Spirit of America Award. His newest show, *Shrek the Musical* (book and lyrics) premiered at Seattle's 5th Avenue Theater, and opened on Broadway. His other works include *Fuddy Meers*, *Kimberly Akimbo*, *Wonder of the World*, *High Fidelity*, and *A Devil Inside*, among others. In addition to his work in theatre, David wrote the screenplay for the Newline feature *Inkheart*, and Sony Picture's upcoming *Spider-Man 4*. David is also currently at work on screen adaptations of his plays *Rabbit Hole* for 20th Century Fox, starring Nicole Kidman, and *Kimberly Akimbo* for Killer Films and DreamWorks. He is a proud New Dramatists alum, a graduate of Sarah Lawrence College and the Juilliard School, as well as a member of the WGA and the Dramatists Guild Council.

## ACKNOWLEDGMENTS

*That Other Person* was originally produced by The 24 Hour Company as part of *The 24 Hour Plays on Broadway*, a one-night-only benefit for Working Playground, Inc., at the Roundabout Theater in New York City on October 24, 2005. It was directed by Christopher Ashley with the following cast:

| | |
|---|---|
| TAPPY | Elizabeth Berkley |
| JACK | Andrew McCarthy |
| GINGE | Cady Huffman |
| KEVIN | Cheyenne Jackson |
| SISSY | Rachel Dratch |

## CAST OF CHARACTERS

All in their mid thirties.

TAPPY, sweet, beautiful, thin, and can't swim

JACK, a man with regrets in search of hope

GINGE, an occasionally mean woman who never stands up

KEVIN, a guy, in every sense of the word

SISSY, a generally good-natured lady who has been pushed too far tonight

## SET

Interior: A beautiful home somewhere in Connecticut.

## THE STORY

Tonight is the night Ginge and Kevin are going to tell their respective spouses the marriage-shattering secret they've been keeping from everyone. But their bomb-shell gets put on the back-burner when a gorgeous peeping-tom, with secrets of her own, falls in the pool and nearly drowns.

# THAT OTHER PERSON

*Lights up on a really nice house in Connecticut.* TAPPY *sits, sopping wet. Her clothes are wet. Her hair is wet. There is a puddle of water at her feet. She looks around uncomfortably.*

KEVIN *and* JACK *stand nearby trying to figure her out.* GINGE, *as always, is sitting. She stays seated through the whole play. We have a couple beats of silence before* TAPPY *speaks…*

**TAPPY.** You know who's a good swimmer? My son. Sawyer. You don't know him, but he's a very good swimmer. My parents have a pool, so he was swimming when he was like…three. So cute.

> *(Beat.)*

He's fifteen now. Believe it or not. And not so cute anymore. He sniffs paint out of paper bags. Last week he mugged a deaf girl. Ya gotta wonder. What happened to that other person. The one I liked. Ya know?

**JACK.** Are you alright? You seem a little…

**TAPPY.** Well yeah, obviously. Because I can't swim. Good thing that ladder was there.

**JACK.** Can't swim?

**TAPPY.** Never learned. I was always too scared of being seen in a bathing suit.

**KEVIN.** *(Finds this hard to believe:)* Really?

**JACK.** Sissy'll be back in a minute with the towels.

**TAPPY.** Thanks.

> *(Looks around.)*

It's a lovely home.

**JACK.** Oh thank you. We just renovated.

**TAPPY.** It's nice. I like the little kitchen area there.

**GINGE.** Can I ask what you were doing just now?

**TAPPY.** Oh, you mean the—

> *(Motions out back.)*

**GINGE.** Yeah.

**TAPPY.** It was so silly actually. But I was hiding. In the—those plant things—I don't know what they're called.

**GINGE.** The hydrangeas?

**TAPPY.** I don't know. I'm not really good with names of plants. Plus it was dark, so— But I was hiding in the…hydrangeas, I guess—trying to look in the windows. To spy on you. And then I heard someone coming.

121

**KEVIN.** That was me. Stepping out for a smoke.

**TAPPY.** You should quit.

**KEVIN.** Yeah, well.

**TAPPY.** Anyway, I got spooked, so I ran, but I didn't really know where I was going, so that's when I tripped over the garden gnome and fell in the pool.

**JACK.** *(Beat.)* Right.

**GINGE.** So, um…why were you spying on us?

**TAPPY.** Oh, I shouldn't have said spying. It's not like I was—

**GINGE.** Jack, I think we should call the police.

**TAPPY.** No, it's okay. Really, it's okay. Because I know you.

*(Pause as they stare at her.)*

I know you. And you know me. You know me, so it's okay.

**GINGE.** We don't know you.

**TAPPY.** Yes you do.

**KEVIN.** We don't. *I* don't.

**GINGE.** And it's against the law to peek into people's windows.

**TAPPY.** I wanted to make sure it was the right address. The internet can be unreliable, so…

**GINGE.** *(Re: the police:)* Jack, can you please…

**TAPPY.** You just don't recognize me because of the operation.

*(This silences them.)*

That's why you think you don't know me. I had an operation.

*(SISSY comes down the stairs carrying towels.)*

**SISSY.** I'm sorry, I had trouble finding the towels. I know you said the first closet on the right, Ginge, but I got all turned around. I mean, you have so many closets up there it's hard to get your bearings, especially when my head is so—

*(She makes an "everything's nuts" expression.)*

Here you go.

*(Hands towels to TAPPY.)*

**TAPPY.** Thank you.

**SISSY.** I spent like five minutes in the linen closet before I realized "oh wait, this is the *linen* closet, she said '*Not* the linen closet.'" And then there was *another* closet which was filled with cloth *napkins,* which was kinda odd, because I was like "Wow, Ginge has a *napkin* Closet. I don't know anyone with a *napkin* closet." So weird.

**GINGE.** But you found them.

**SISSY.** Yeah, I found them.

*(Beat—bursts into tears.)*

I'm sorry. I'm sorry. I'm still thinking about… I'm sorry.

*(More crying. Awkward pause.)*

**TAPPY.** Aw geez, I interrupted something, didn't I?

**OTHERS.** *(Ad lib:)* No, not really. Actually… Really, no. etc.

**TAPPY.** No, I did. She's crying. Plus I saw you arguing when I was spying in the…

*(Motions out back.)*

**JACK.** Hydrangeas.

**TAPPY.** Hydrangeas, thank you. That's why I stayed put for so long. Otherwise I might've just rung the bell.

**SISSY.** *(Wipes her eyes.)* You were spying on us?

*(Turns to KEVIN.)*

Is this about—? She doesn't have anything to do with you and—?

**KEVIN.** No, of course not. What would she have to do with that?

**SISSY.** I don't know! How *would* I know?! You're so full of fucking *lies! Anything* is possible!

**TAPPY.** *(Beat.)* I am, I'm interrupting.

**SISSY.** It's fine. You didn't know. Or maybe you *did*. Who *are* you?!

**GINGE.** She says we know her, but we don't recognize her because she's had an operation.

**SISSY.** Oh. An operation.

**KEVIN.** Was it plastic surgery?

**TAPPY.** No.

**SISSY.** I leave the room for a few minutes—

*(Turns on GINGE viciously.)*

If you didn't have so many *fucking* closets I'd know what was going on right now.

**GINGE.** You need to stop swearing, Sissy.

**SISSY.** And you need to stop fucking my husband!

*(Bursts into tears again.)*

**KEVIN.** Oh for god sakes, Sissy.

**TAPPY.** Is that what this is? You two just told those two that you were… Well this is really awkward then. Me falling in the pool in the middle of all this. My timing has always has been lousy. Remember?

**GINGE.** We don't know who you are!

**TAPPY.** Sure you do. Remember that time at the thing with the…cotton candy machine? And the monkey?

*(Off their blank stares.)*

And the dwarf…with the…thermos…

*(Still nothing.)*

You guys, it's *me*. Tappy. Tappy Reynolds. *Tappy.*

*(Pause.)*

See? I know you.

**SISSY.** Me? You know me?

**TAPPY.** Well no, not you. But you seem very nice.

**SISSY.** Thank you. I *am* nice.

*(Turns on her husband.)*

I am a nice person, who deserves to be treated with a modicum of respect!

**TAPPY.** We all went to high school together.

**SISSY.** Cool.

**KEVIN.** You're not Tappy Reynolds. Tappy Reynolds was enormous.

**TAPPY.** Yeah, was. *Was* enormous.

**KEVIN.** Like three hundred pounds.

**TAPPY.** Three fifteen. I got the operation.

**SISSY.** The Al Roker operation?

**TAPPY.** Well, that's not the official name, but yeah.

**GINGE.** You're not Tappy.

**JACK.** No, she *is*. I can see it now. Now that I look at her.

**KEVIN.** You look amazing.

**TAPPY.** Thank you.

**KEVIN.** Damn, I wish you looked like that in high school.

**TAPPY.** Yeah, me too.

**SISSY.** You know, our dog is obese. They don't do that operation on dogs, do they?

**TAPPY.** I don't think so.

**GINGE.** So what do you want Tappy? You come back to show us how great you look?

**TAPPY.** No.

**GINGE.** Some kind of revenge thing? "Hey, look at me now, assholes."?

**TAPPY.** No, not at all.

*(Beat—has to admit:)*

Well not, *just* that…

*(No one really laughs.)*

Although…you were pretty mean to me, Ginge. Remember? The locker room? The tub of Bosco?

**GINGE.** We were kids. Kids are mean.

**JACK.** No they're not. Not all kids. I wasn't mean.

**TAPPY.** That's true, Jack wasn't mean.

**SISSY.** But Ginge was. She's *still* mean. She slept with my husband. While I was at a clinic getting my varicose veins done.

**KEVIN.** Sissy, give it a rest.

**SISSY.** *(Teary again:)* I was getting those veins done for you, Kevin! So my calves would look pretty for you!

*(Suddenly:)*

I want a divorce!

**GINGE.** Good, so does he.

**SISSY.** *(To GINGE:)* You're mean. You're mean to me, and to your husband, and to Tappy. You were very mean to Tappy.

*(To TAPPY:)*

Well God got her back for you, Tap. Did you notice how it was *me* who had to fetch the towels? Or how she hasn't gotten out of that chair *once*? That's because she's a paraplegic. Dune buggy accident! Four years ago. Her wheelchair's in the hall, wanna see?

**KEVIN.** Don't be a jackass, Sissy.

**SISSY.** Why not? Everyone else gets to be mean. Why not me?

**JACK.** I'm not mean.

**TAPPY.** *(To GINGE:)* I'm sorry.

**GINGE.** Oh shut up. Please.

**SISSY.** See?! Mean! Mean-mean-mean. Kevin is only having sex with you because he has an overdeveloped sense of guilt when it comes to the handicapped. He had a retarded sister and she died choking on a piece of hotdog because he didn't know the Heimlich!

**KEVIN.** Jesus, Sissy!

**SISSY.** Too bad! I'm done being nice! We're getting a divorce, so fuck off!

**JACK.** *(To TAPPY:)* Is it your son? Sawyer? Is that why you're here?

**TAPPY.** *(Pause.)* He's having a hard time.

**SISSY.** She has a son?

**GINGE.** He sniffs paint. You were upstairs.

**TAPPY.** I know I said I'd never do this, Jack. But I don't know what to do with him. And he keeps asking about you. I think he blames you for…everything. I'm sorry, but I think he does.

**GINGE.** Uhhh…what the fuck?

**TAPPY.** You never told her?

**JACK.** We said we wouldn't tell anyone.

**GINGE.** What the FUCK?

**SISSY.** You need to stop swearing, Ginge.

**KEVIN.** Dude, do you have a kid?

**TAPPY.** We slept together *once.* I was a freshman. He was drunk,

**JACK.** I wasn't *that* drunk.

**TAPPY.** Drunk enough to fuck the fat girl.

**JACK.** Hey, it wasn't like that. I liked you. You were sweet.

**TAPPY.** Yeah, right.

> *(To GINGE:)*

Why do you think I left school?

**GINGE.** Because your family moved or something.

**TAPPY.** Yeah, because I was pregnant. Jack didn't want any part of it, obviously, which I totally understood. He was going off to Dartmouth. I promised not to get in his way.

**GINGE.** *(To JACK:)* Okay, this is insanity. We've been married for *eleven years—*

**JACK.** Tappy and I had an agreement. She said I wouldn't have to— It was like it didn't happen for me.

**GINGE.** Right, but...

> *(Motions to TAPPY.)*

It kinda did, Jack.

**TAPPY.** *(To JACK:)* I'm sorry. I didn't know what else to do. I'm afraid he's gonna die. He's doing the craziest shit. And he hates me. He hates everybody really. He's a delight. You're gonna love him.

**JACK.** So you want me to what? Like...talk to him? Cause I'm not so good at that kind of thing.

**TAPPY.** I think just meeting him might be good.

**JACK.** *(Pause—lets out a breath.)* Okay.

**GINGE.** Jack—

**JACK.** When?

**TAPPY.** How 'bout now?

**SISSY.** Wait, we were in the middle of something, what is this?

**TAPPY.** I parked down the hill.

**JACK.** He's in the car?

**GINGE.** Jack, you are not bringing that boy in this house. He'll probably torch the place by the sounds of it. And we just renovated.

**JACK.** What do you care? You're leaving, right? Isn't that what tonight was about?

*(To* TAPPY*:)*

Why don't you go get him? I wanna meet him.

**TAPPY.** Okay.

*(Smiles.)*

Let me go talk with him, I'll bring him up.

*(To* GINGE*:)*

And he's not gonna torch anything. Jesus.

*(Exits.)*

**SISSY.** Well, we are obviously being kicked out. This has been a banner night, honestly. I'm getting my coat.

**KEVIN.** Dude, I'm sorry about the other stuff. With Ginge.

**JACK.** No, you did me a favor. There hasn't been anything for years. Before the accident even. I only stayed with her because I felt bad for her.

**GINGE.** That's lovely. Thanks, Jack.

**JACK.** Well Jesus, you despise me, Ginge. What do you want me to say?

*(To* KEVIN*:)*

She's all yours.

**SISSY.** And just so you all know, I'm putting all of this on my blog.

*(To* KEVIN*:)*

I'm taking the car. You can fuckin' walk.

*(Storms out.)*

**KEVIN.** Hey baby, don't be like that.

*(Goes out after her.)*

*(*GINGE *and* JACK *are silent for a couple beats.)*

**GINGE.** I wasn't always mean, Jack. You know that.

*(Beat.)*

We used to laugh all the time.

**JACK.** Yeah, at other people. That's what you found funny.

**GINGE.** Not always. What about that track meet in Darien. When the bus broke down. And then the truck with the pigs pulled over. I was just…funny. You called me Shecky for like the rest of the semester. Remember?

**JACK.** No. I mean, I know it happened, but…no.

*(She just stares at him.)*

**JACK.** When they come in, tell them to meet me out back.

**GINGE.** Where are you going?

**JACK.** I'm taking a dip in the pool.

*(Goes off.)*

**GINGE.** *(Calls after him:)* Can you at least get my chair please? Jack?
  *(No response.)*
Jack?
  *(No response.)*
Jack?
  *(But he doesn't come back.* GINGE *is left stranded, as the lights fade.)*

*End of Play*

# THE SUNDAY TIMES
## by Terrence McNally

# BIOGRAPHY

Terrence McNally's most recent collaboration is the book for *The Visit* at Arlington's Signature Theatre with score by John Kander and Fredd Ebb. His most recent play *Unusual Acts of Devotion* premiered at the Philadelphia Theatre Company in 2008. His play *Deuce* played on Broadway in the 2006-2007 season. His play *Some Men* premiered in the 2007 season at Second Stage Theatre. Mr. McNally also recently wrote the books for the musicals *Chita Rivera: The Dancer's Life* and *Man of No Importance*. Recent Broadway credits include the revival of his play *The Ritz*, the revival of *Frankie and Johnny in the Clair de Lune* and the book for the musical *The Full Monty*. He won his fourth Tony Award for Best Book of a Musical for *Ragtime* (music and lyrics by Stephen Flaherty and Lynn Ahrens). Mr. McNally won the Tony in 1996 for his play *Master Class,* in which Zoe Caldwell created the role of Maria Callas; the 1995 Tony, Drama Desk and Outer Critics Circle Awards for Best Play as well as the New York Drama Critics' Circle Award for Best American Play for *Love! Valour! Compassion!*; and the 1993 Tony for his book of the musical *Kiss of the Spiderwoman* (music and lyrics by Kander and Ebb). His other plays include *Dedication or The Stuff of Dreams*; *The Stendhal Syndrome*; *Crucifixion*; *Corpus Christi*; *A Perfect Ganesh*; *Lips Together, Teeth Apart*; *The Lisbon Traviata* and *It's Only a Play*, all of which began at the Manhattan Theatre Club. Earlier stage works include *Bad Habits, Where Has Tommy Flowers Gone?, Things That Go Bump in the Night, Next* and the book for the musical *The Rink* (music and lyrics by Kander and Ebb). For the Central Park Opera trilogy presented at the New York City Opera in the fall of 1999, he wrote the libretto for *The Food of Love*, with music by Robert Beaser. The San Francisco Opera presented *Dead Man Walking* with Mr. McNally's libretto and music by Jake Heggie. Mr. McNally has written a number of TV scripts, including *Andre's Mother* for which he won an Emmy Award. He has received two Guggenheim Fellowships, a Rockefeller Grant, a Lucille Lortel Award, and a citation from the American Academy of Arts and Letters. He has been a member of the Dramatists Guild since 1970.

## ACKNOWLEDGMENTS

*The Sunday Times* was originally produced by The 24 Hour Company as a part of *The 24 Hour Plays on Broadway* at The American Airlines Theatre on October 23, 2006. It was directed by Miguel Arteta with the following cast:

SUSAN ........................................................................ Amy Ryan
RICHARD ............................................................. Liev Schreiber
PETER .............................................................. Pablo Schreiber
LOGAN ................................................................ Michael Ealy

## CAST OF CHARACTERS

SUSAN
RICHARD
PETER
LOGAN

# THE SUNDAY TIMES

A large living room in a well-appointed country house. SUSAN, RICHARD, PETER, *and* LOGAN *are reading the Sunday* New York Times. *The room is awash in various sections of it.* SUSAN *and* RICHARD *are married.* PETER *and* LOGAN *are married.* PETER *and* SUSAN *are brother and sister. Long silence while everyone reads their favorite section.*

**SUSAN.** There is just so much shit in the air lately. I'm suffocating on it.

**RICHARD.** You don't suffocate on shit, Susan, you choke on it. Are you through with the Real Estate section?

*(PETER passes it to him.)*

**SUSAN.** What are we doing about it? Huh? Tell me, what?

**PETER.** What are we doing about what?

**SUSAN.** The shit.

**LOGAN.** There are no same sex or interracial couples in the Wedding Section this week either.

**PETER.** That makes three in a row.

**SUSAN.** This is exactly what I'm talking about.

**LOGAN.** Same sex and interracial couples are not part of the shit you're talking about, Susan.

**SUSAN.** Everything is part of the shit I'm talking about. You, me, Peter, my husband, this room, this house, this weekend, this country—it suddenly came to me: we are all fucked—figuratively, literally and royally fucked. This is supposed to be a great country—at least I think that was the original intention. And it was a great country.

**RICHARD.** Sentimental!

**SUSAN.** All right, it was on the cusp of greatness.

**RICHARD.** And you're on the cusp of sentimental.

**PETER.** My sister hates to be sentimental and wants Richard to tell her anytime she is.

**RICHARD.** My wife hates to be sentimental and wants me to tell her anytime she is, Peter. Tell your partner other human beings are still in the same room, will you, Logan?

**LOGAN.** Peter is not my partner, Richard. Peter is my husband, Peter is my spouse. How many times must I remind you of that?

**RICHARD.** I stand corrected.

**LOGAN.** You talk the talk but I have the feeling you are profoundly, narcissistically homophobic.

**RICHARD.** Why narcissistically?

**LOGAN.** You think we want you.

**RICHARD.** Some of you do. I have my admirers.

**LOGAN.** In your dreams maybe.

**RICHARD.** No, there's this guy at my—.

**SUSAN.** Why do I feel like I'm talking to myself?

**RICHARD.** I'm sorry, Susan had the floor.

**SUSAN.** I was talking about being on the edge of something but—and tell me if I'm crazy—it seems like five minutes ago, it stopped, dead in its tracks, and we stopped with it.

**LOGAN.** What stopped?

**SUSAN.** We did, this country. All of a sudden, just like that, somebody turned the lights out.

**PETER.** You're not crazy, Suzie.

**LOGAN.** It's true. Your sister's right. She is, Richard. You have a point, Sue.

**SUSAN.** I have a what? A point? I am burning with rage and you tell me I have a point. You make me want to slap you in the face, Logan.

**RICHARD.** Susan's research grant at the hospital wasn't renewed.

**SUSAN.** Don't explain me in a couple of words. I'm not that simple.

**RICHARD.** I wasn't suggesting you were, darling.

**SUSAN.** And don't patronize me. I'm your fucking wife who's born you two children, for Christ's sake.

**RICHARD.** I wasn't patronizing you, Susan.

**SUSAN.** I'm sorry, all of you, my humble apologies. I used to be nice. I got tired of it. There was nothing to be nice about. The girl at the A&P said "It's always a pleasure to see your smiling face" one time too many and I just lost it right there in the Express Check Out lane. I started screaming at her, "I have 19 items in my basket and the limit is 15." I am taking advantage of who I am. I am ignoring your pathetic little sign. I am acting superior to you. I am not superior to you. I am not superior to anyone and what is this ridiculous game we are all playing. We are living in a house of cards. When will it fall down? Somebody, please, make it fall down. All men are equal. All men are brothers. The truth of that is gnawing at my innards more viciously than any cancer we cannot find the cure for at my hospital.

*(RICHARD takes his wife in his arms.)*

**RICHARD.** I couldn't love anyone as much as I love you, even the boys. Is that a terrible thing to say?

**SUSAN.** It's a ridiculous thing.

**RICHARD.** If someone laid a finger on either one of them, I would crush his skull between these two hands until it cracked open and his brain and blood and protoplasm gushed forth and I was drenched in them.

**LOGAN.** I hope you're not looking at me when you say that.

**RICHARD.** We'll make it all right again, Susan, like it was, just you, me, and the boys. We don't need anyone or anything.

**PETER.** Yes, you do, Richard. We all need one another.

**LOGAN.** What does your brother-in-law say, Peter? "Sentimental"!

**PETER.** It's true, we do. We need one another or we die.

**LOGAN.** You have me.

**PETER.** I need more than you.

**LOGAN.** It's a start.

**PETER.** It's not enough.

**LOGAN.** Don't say that.

**PETER.** It's true. And you need more than me.

**LOGAN.** I'm very happy.

**PETER.** You know what I'm saying.

**RICHARD.** It looks like we both have our hands full, Peter.

**LOGAN.** I love Peter, Peter loves me.

**RICHARD.** I've been trying to tell this woman the same thing.

**PETER.** My sister is the bravest person I know. When we were little she'd beat the shit out of the kids who bullied me.

**SUSAN.** I shouldn't have stopped.

**PETER.** There was no need to. I grew up and could fend for myself.

**SUSAN.** That is such a sissy, insipid, bullshit-homosexual word: fend! It makes me want to beat you up, Peter.

**RICHARD.** Don't worry, I'll take care of your sister for you, Peter.

**SUSAN.** I hope you men are doing a lot more than fending for yourself or you'll never get the rights you say you want. You, too, my raging heterosexual stud husband.

**RICHARD.** Look who's lightening up!

**SUSAN.** Don't make fun, Rich. Please, please, please don't make fun.

**RICHARD.** I wasn't, honest.

**SUSAN.** I can only stay in that place where I was so long until I think "If I don't get out of here, I'm going to kill myself."

**RICHARD.** I don't blame you. There's a name for that place. Righteousness. No one can live there.

**SUSAN.** It's not righteousness.

**RICHARD.** It sure sounds like it.

**SUSAN.** It's hopelessness. Nothing changes. Can or will change. We're fucked. We're fucked with our Lexus in the driveway. Our boys are fucked on their fast track to the university of their choice. Our country is fucked above and beyond any particular Administration. They'll find the cure for cancer before they find the cure for the shit we're drowning in. I was in the attic last weekend and I found my high school annual. Someone had written in it: "To Susan of the luminous smile." It's not luminous anymore.

**RICHARD.** To me it is.

**SUSAN.** Sentimental!

**PETER.** The other night in the city Logan and I were walking hand in hand, which is our wont when we're in a safe neighborhood...

**SUSAN.** You wont!

**RICHARD.** Sssshh.

**SUSAN.** I'm sorry, it's so limp.

**PETER.** It's just a word, Suzie.

**SUSAN.** They're all we have sometimes.

**RICHARD.** Shut up and listen to what he's *saying*. Fuck his words.

**PETER.** Thank you, raging heterosexual stud.

**LOGAN.** We were near 11th Street where it dead-ends into the church-seminary-school-crap thing they got there.

**PETER.** Logan hates organized religion.

**LOGAN.** And we were holding hands...

**PETER.** ...Which remains our wont...!

**LOGAN.** When we saw this gang coming towards us. Noisy, loud, high. Mostly black.

**PETER.** A couple of them had bats.

**LOGAN.** One had a golf stick.

**PETER.** And he wasn't Tiger Woods.

**LOGAN.** I looked at Peter.

**PETER.** I looked at Logan.

**LOGAN.** And we held hands even harder. Fuck them!

**PETER.** Fuck them, we said.

**LOGAN.** They walked right by us. And they saw what we were doing. They couldn't miss it. They didn't give a shit. Can you believe it?

**PETER.** So some things are getting better. We're fucked but not *as* fucked, Suzie, huh?

**SUSAN.** We're fucked.

**RICHARD.** I dreamed I was a woman the other night. A big gorgeous voluptuous woman. It was so cool. I had tits like watermelons and fabulously plump but firm thighs that tapered down into the most slender, delicate, beautiful ankles you ever saw. I was wearing black patent leather pumps with stiletto heels. That's all I was wearing. I don't know what had happened to my dick. It was gone. I guess that's what happens when you dream you're a woman. Anyway, I was dangerous. I was looking for trouble. I had a riding crop and I was just kind of tapping it on my right hip, waiting for some action. I wanted to whup someone with it something fierce. But then I felt this pain in my stomach, something terrible, my knees buckled from it, and there I was in the gutter, rolling in agony, holding myself in a ball, when I started giving birth. I thought I had been split open. The pain was so keen, I was crying from it. Child after child was born. They kept coming out. They wouldn't stop. The pain was terrific but so was the elation. I felt good. I felt right. I liked being a mother. When I woke up, Susan was holding me. My pillow and the hair on my chest were drenched in my tears.

**SUSAN.** He told me about the dream *after* we made love.

**RICHARD.** The day you don't turn me on is the day I drop dead.

**LOGAN.** Sentimental!

*(The two couples take stock of their respective partners and are well pleased with what they see.)*

**PETER.** I love you, Logan.

**LOGAN.** I know.

**PETER.** That's it, you know?

**LOGAN.** What do you want me to say?

**RICHARD.** I love you, Susan.

**SUSAN.** I still say, we're fucked.

*(The men begin to read the paper again.)*

**PETER.** Who has the Arts and Leisure section?

**RICHARD.** The Sunday *Times* always upsets you.

**LOGAN.** Is Leslie a woman's name?

**RICHARD.** It can be.

**LOGAN.** Then we have a couple of lesbians who got married.

**SUSAN.** Fucked.

**PETER.** *(Re-attacking the crosswords puzzle:)* I need a six-letter word for "state of mind."

**SUSAN.** Fucked, fucked, fucked.

**PETER.** Thank you, sis!

**LOGAN.** Patent leather pumps, huh?

**RICHARD.** I was gorgeous. Eat your heart out, Logan.

**SUSAN.** Fucked.

*End of Play*

# POOR BOB
## by Elizabeth Meriwether

## BIOGRAPHY

Elizabeth Meriwether's play *The Mistakes Madeline Made* was originally produced by Naked Angels Theater, and was subsequently produced at Yale Rep and published by Dramatists Play Service. Her other plays include *Heddatron*, an adaptation of *Hedda Gabler* featuring live robots which was produced by Les Freres Corbusier, and is published by Playscripts, Inc.; *Nicky Goes Goth*, which was first produced in 2004 in the New York Fringe Festival; and *Oliver*, which will be workshopped by the Vineyard Theatre. Ms. Meriwether is currently working on commissions from the Yale Repertory Theatre, Ars Nova, and Manhattan Theatre Club.

## ACKNOWLEDGMENTS

*Poor Bob* was originally produced by The 24 Hour Company at The Signature Theater on the set of *The Trip to Bountiful* in New York City on December 5, 2005. It was directed by Mark Armstrong and featured the following cast:

SEYMOUR ............................................................. Michael Esper
KITTY .................................................................... Krysten Ritter
NOAH .................................................................. Matt Stadelmann
BOB ...................................................................... Patrick Heusinger

## CAST OF CHARACTERS

SEYMOUR
KITTY
NOAH
BOB

# Poor Bob

SEYMOUR, KITTY, *and* NOAH *sit looking at the* Yahtzee *box.*

**KITTY.** Still red. Untouched by the sun.

*(A moment.)*

**SEYMOUR.** Say it—

**NOAH.** Oh shit.

**KITTY.** Oh shit.

**SEYMOUR.** Yiggity-yahtzee.

**KITTY.** Yow-tzee.

**NOAH.** Copyright by Milton Bradley in 1982—1990—and then again in—

**KITTY.** Again—

**NOAH.** In 1996.

**SEYMOUR.** Nineteen. Ninety. Siiiiiiix.

*(A moment.)*

I want to die with a dice cup. Like. In my hand. Like gripping it.

**KITTY.** Like the death grip.

**SEYMOUR.** I want my death grip to be like on a Yahtzee dice cup.

**NOAH.** Whoa.

**KITTY.** What?

**NOAH.** No—it's just. It's just. Wow. What do I want my death grip on? Like what is it—what is the THING that I want to be GRIPPING when I DIE?

**SEYMOUR.** That's huge.

**NOAH.** I think it's huge.

**SEYMOUR.** They're going to have to pry it out of my hands.

**NOAH.** Who's going to pry it?

**KITTY.** You think the police are going to pry a Yahtzee dice cup out of your hands?

**SEYMOUR.** Yeah. Yeah. CSI Miami. That's like somebody's job to pry it out your fingers—I want it to be like IMPOSSIBLE. TO. GET IT OUT! I want them to like have to get the hammer—

**NOAH.** I don't know.

**KITTY.** What?

**NOAH.** I don't know. I think I want. Like. I think I want my wife to do it. Like whoever's going to be my wife. I want to be holding her hand. And then I don't want anyone to pry us apart.

(*NOAH stares at* KITTY.)

I want that to be my death grip.

(*A moment.*)

**KITTY.** You look so familiar.

**SEYMOUR.** You met him on move-in day.

**NOAH.** You got me water. It was: Cold. It was: Cold. Water.

**SEYMOUR.** He's like my best friend now. And he loves Yahtzee like almost as much as you do. Which makes him like my home away from home.

**KITTY.** No—it's from before—there's something before—

**SEYMOUR.** Where's that guy who was following you around? Bob?

**KITTY.** He's like—I don't know. Wandering the hallways.

**SEYMOUR.** You don't love him.

**KITTY.** I don't know.

**SEYMOUR.** You want me to do the gag thing?

**KITTY.** No! I don't know. No! I have to settle down. I have to stop chasing after—you know—

**NOAH.** Who?

**SEYMOUR.** Atreyu.

**NOAH.** What?

**SEYMOUR.** Like Neverending Story.

**KITTY.** Like little boy who saves the world of imagination from the Nothing.

**SEYMOUR.** She's got like a thing.

**KITTY.** I've got an Atreyu thing. I don't want to talk about it.

**SEYMOUR.** She like purchased this game of Yahtzee on the internet because apparently Atreyu like touched it during the filming or some shit.

**KITTY.** I know everything. Like in German Neverending Story is Die Unendliche Geschichte.

**NOAH.** (*Overlapping:*) Geschichte.

**KITTY.** Whoa.

**NOAH.** Die Unendliche Geschichte.

(*BOB enters.*)

**BOB.** Baaaabe.

**KITTY.** Oh god.

**BOB.** (*To* NOAH:) I'm Bob. (*To* SEYMOUR:) I'm Bob.

**KITTY.** Shut up Bob! PLEASE SHUT UP!

(*KITTY starts to sob.*)

**BOB.** *(To* SEYMOUR:*)* So—are you Kitty's brother? I've heard a lot about you. It's great to finally meet you.

**KITTY.** *(Sobbing uncontrollably:)* Oh god—oh god—Atreyu—ATREYU—

**SEYMOUR.** This is bullshit. I'm doing the gag thing!

**BOB.** What?

**NOAH.** Sometimes she…sometimes she just starts crying…and apparently he has to gag her…

(SEYMOUR *starts gagging her.)*

**BOB.** Babe? Are you okay with this?

(KITTY *gives the thumb's up.* SEYMOUR *gags her.)*

**SEYMOUR.** Jesus Christ. Silence. I can't believe you've never had to gag her. Doesn't she cry all the time?

**BOB.** Yeah.

**SEYMOUR.** What do you do—you just let her cry?

**BOB.** I use that time to catch up on my emails.

**NOAH.** Hey— Are you okay now?

(KITTY *nods. Smiles.* NOAH *smiles back at her.)*

**BOB.** Thanks for. Letting us crash here. I know the dorm room is like a sacred space. That's what I remember. You know. From Harvard.

**SEYMOUR.** You've got a turkey hat. I think that's great Bob. That shit is so real. Put it on.

**NOAH.** Put it on Bob.

**BOB.** Oh. Okay.

**SEYMOUR.** Wow. Look at that.

**BOB.** It's just—a couple of my buddies—

**NOAH.** Look at that.

**BOB.** So you…went through my bag?

**SEYMOUR.** She's my sister. Of course I'm going to go through your bag. Of course that's what I'm going to do.

**BOB.** No I get it. Totally. The protective thing. I'm totally down with that.

**SEYMOUR.** You think it's weird. It's not weird. It would be weird if I was like looking at your balls.

**BOB.** What?

**NOAH.** Seymour's always like 3 words away from saying balls.

**SEYMOUR.** Just recently. I just like sort of recently discovered how many times the word "balls" can be used in a sentence.

**BOB.** Ha.-ha. Balls. Baaaaalls. Yeah!

*(Silence.)*

I haven't really met you yet—

**NOAH.** Noah.

**SEYMOUR.** I love Noah. He's like my best friend. I love everything about him. Look at his hair. I love his hair.

**NOAH.** Oh shit man—I love your hair.

**BOB.** *(It's a joke:)* Do you love my hair?

**SEYMOUR.** Yeah sure we do Bob. I love you. I totally love you. It's crazy how much I love you Bob.

**BOB.** Well I. I love your sister.

**SEYMOUR.** Yeah. Yeah. Baaaahb. Let's talk about that. What do you think?

**BOB.** Okay.

**SEYMOUR.** Okay. Why do you think my sister is crying Bob?

**BOB.** I don't—I don't know.

**SEYMOUR.** Huh. Huuuuh. I'm stumped.

**BOB.** Sometimes she cries...I just put her in a room by herself and she usually stops.

**SEYMOUR.** Is that something that a happy girl does—Bob?

**BOB.** Uh.

**SEYMOUR.** I don't see Happy here—do you see Happy? I see a turkey hat but I don't see happy.

**BOB.** I—I don't

**SEYMOUR.** So let's think about that for a second Bob. Let's just do some thinking together. Hmmm… Hmmm… Hmmm…

*(A moment.)*

**BOB.** It's me. I'm not making her happy.

**SEYMOUR.** Oh. Wow. Wow. You said it.

**BOB.** Kitty? Am I not making you happy?

*(KITTY shakes her head.)*

Oh. Oh god.

*(A silence.)*

Maybe I'll go set up my bed. Is there like a futon?

*(A moment.)*

There's gotta be a futon… Everyone has a futon…

*(A moment.)*

I'll go find the futon.

*(BOB exits. A moment.)*

**NOAH.** We don't have a futon.

**SEYMOUR.** He's like devastated. That's like: Devastation. You got to go after him.

*(KITTY takes the gag off.)*

**KITTY.** I've got a couple minutes. Right? We could get a game in.

**SEYMOUR.** I can't keep doing the gag thing. I'm in college now. Things have to change.

**KITTY.** It's the last time—I promise. I promise. I'm going to make it work with him. I'm gonna. I gonna grow up. I'm going to figure out how to love someone. I just need to take these 5 minutes I have left of my childhood to play some Yahtzee before the nothing comes and eats everything…okay? Before the nothing comes…

*(A moment.)*

**BOB'S VOICE.** *(In agony:)* Looks like there's no futon!

**SEYMOUR.** This is so depressing. I've got to make him some soup or some shit.

*(SEYMOUR exits.)*

**KITTY.** What? You think I'm crazy?

**NOAH.** Me? No. No.

**KITTY.** You think it's crazy that I use my little brother to break up with my boyfriends because I'm obsessed with Arteyu from Neverending Story? Because I could see how you could think that's crazy.

**NOAH.** I—I don't.

**KITTY.** I've got to move on. I've got to stop THIS. I've got to move the fuck on. I've gotta love this guy. He's a good guy. He's. He's got really big shoulders.

**NOAH.** They are really big.

**KITTY.** They're really big! And he loves me! I'm lucky! I'm lucky to be loved. At some point you have to stop taking love for granted. The love people give you.

**NOAH.** I guess. I guess so.

*(KITTY holds the Yahtzee Box.)*

**KITTY.** And then. He touched this box. Or I don't know—that's what it said on eBay. And I believed it. I just believe. I just keep believing… It's like I can't stop myself…

**NOAH.** Are you going to start crying again?

**KITTY.** No. No.

*(KITTY put the box down.)*

This is ridiculous. I'm a ridiculous person.

(SEYMOUR *enters.*)

**SEYMOUR.** He's hitting himself in the head with a saucepan. You got to talk to him Noah. It needs the Noah Hathaway touch.

**KITTY.** Noah Hathaway.

**SEYMOUR.** Noah Hathaway. That's his name.

(SEYMOUR *exits.*)

**KITTY.** Noah Hathaway?

**NOAH.** Kitty—

**KITTY.** Noah Hathaway. Noah Hathaway born on November 13. You're one-quarter Mohegan. Your middle name is Leslie.

**NOAH.** Kitty—

(KITTY *falls to her knees.*)

**KITTY.** Atreyu…Atreyu…

**NOAH.** I can't. I can't do it anymore. It was so long ago. I was just a child actor.

**KITTY.** Atreyu. Please.

(*A moment.*)

I'm deathly ill…Atreyu…

**NOAH.** I'll save you. The princess of Fantasia…

(*They hold each other.*)

I'll save you.

## End of Play

# THE MASTER OF THE WORLD VERSUS THE DUDE

## by Raven Metzner

## BIOGRAPHY

Raven Metzner is a feature screenwriter, television writer, producer and show-runner with over 12 years of experience. Raven has co-written over 10 feature screenplays including *Elektra* and *Deathok* for Marvel Comics Pictures, an adaptation of Don Winslow's *Cool Breeze On The Underground* for Dreamworks, *Nosebleed* for New Line pictures, a comedy titled *The Magnificent Six* for Universal pictures, as well as production rewrites on *Rush Hour 2*. Raven recently co-created, co-wrote and was an Executive Producer for the prime time series *Six Degrees* with ABC television and JJ Abrams' Bad Robot Productions. He is currently developing the DC/Vertigo property *Fables* for Warner Bros. television and ABC as well as the transmedia property *Dragons vs. Robots* with Massiverse, Inc.

## ACKNOWLEDGMENTS

*The Master of the World Versus the Dude* was originally produced by The 24 Hour Company at the Ohio Theatre in New York City on September 3, 1999.

## CAST OF CHARACTERS

D.M.
THE DUDE
SHALIMAR
BETH

# THE MASTER OF THE WORLD
# VERSUS THE DUDE

*A den. The year is 1985. A table and three chairs. Sitting at the head of the table is D.M. He's 17 years old. He's dressed as a normal teenager would dress except he's wearing a silver Nazi battle helmet. In front of him he has a pad, pen, a pile of paper, and some dice.*

*To his right is THE DUDE, also 17. Over his teenager clothes he is wearing a fur tunic. Next to him is SHALIMAR, 16. She is D.M.'s little sister. Over shorts and a t-shirt, she wears a red feather boa and holds a plastic store-bought magic wand.*

*Lights up on a moment of silence. All three of our characters are lost in deep concentration. It's like the final hand of a round of poker.*

**SHALIMAR.** *(Looking to THE DUDE:)* What are you gonna do?

**THE DUDE.** It's a lot of cash.

**SHALIMAR.** It's more cash than we've been able to get our hands on the whole time.

**THE DUDE.** Could you see anything else in there?

**SHALIMAR.** It was dark. I just saw the money. *(Matter of fact:)* ...a LOT of money. Two thousand.

*(D.M. turns slowly, fixes his gaze and centers on THE DUDE.)*

**D.M.** You making a decision?

**SHALIMAR.** I think it's possible.

**D.M.** It's up to... *(Like a marquee title:)* The Dude.

**SHALIMAR.** *(Agreeing:)* It's up to you. You have more experience. I've got no thieving skills...

*(THE DUDE think about it. He really thinks hard.)*

**D.M.** 2000. 2000 golden. 2000 little golden ducats. Shalimar saw it but it's up to you, The Dude, to get it.

**THE DUDE.** I'm thinking.

*(Deciding, standing:)*

Alright, The Dude will sneak in and grab and bag it.

**D.M.** Sneak? You're gonna sneak. Alright. Give me a second.

*(D.M. consults his papers. He picks up the dice and rolls them. He rolls them again. He rolls them again. He sighs.)*

**SHALIMAR.** Is there a chart for sneaking?

*(D.M. and THE DUDE look at her like she's insane. Of course there is! D.M. stands. He waves for THE DUDE to sit.)*

**D.M.** *(A new voice:)* It's midnight. The noises of the deep woods are all around you. In the distance...awoooo! The howl of feral wolves. A crystal moon on the horiz—

**THE DUDE.** D.M. Can you cut the shit and tell me if I snuck successfully?

**D.M.** Can you not be a blow-job for five minutes and let me do my job?

> *(Continuing, the voice:)*

The moonlight lances the night with its crystal talons—

> *(D.M. gets up and acts out suitable portions of this action. THE DUDE watches impatiently. SHALIMAR is mesmerized.)*

—You creep from the bushes where you and the sorceress Shalimar have hidden. Her silky chocolate milk-shake skin reflects the crystal moonlight where the sweat glistens between her breasts.

Across the clearing the faint outline of the tent, you can hear the breathing of the armored men resting around the embers of their campfire. One step...two steps...and CRACK!

> *(Pac-man dying sound:)*

BUSTED! Like Col. Mustard holding custard!

**THE DUDE.** Oh shit! Come on. What happened?

> *(D.M. steps back to the table. He shakes his head, disappointed.)*

**D.M.** Jesus, Dude. You're a barbarian king not a ballerina. Why'd you sneak?

**THE DUDE.** Barbarians can sneak.

**SHALIMAR.** They can! Can't they?

**D.M.** Yeah. Like Attila's Huns snuck down form the North country...like... Conan Sneaks? Does Schwarzenegger pussy foot? It's an impossibility. It's the wrong movie. It's like James Bond in "On Golden Pond."

> *(THE DUDE nods his head. He's taking it like a man.)*

**SHALIMAR.** It's like... It's like..."Scarface" in space?

**THE DUDE.** *(Ignoring her:)* What's the damage?

**D.M.** Nothing you can't handle. 4 ruffians. The king's guard. There's a bug-bear on a chain.

> *(Back in the voice:)*

One of the Ruffians moves to unlock the—

> *(THE DUDE stands. Walks around the room. Big steps.)*

**THE DUDE.** —I'll smite! I'LL SMITE THEM ALL! I'll smite them and take the gold. I'll grab the guy going for the bug-bear and smash his head!

> *(THE DUDE smites the air, two hands clasped into a fist. D.M. sits at the table. He's looking at his pad and rolling dice.)*

**D.M.** You're smiting, right!

**THE DUDE.** *(Really enjoying himself:)* I'm smiting like a bitch!

**D.M.** Alright! You connect! Bam! The guy's head caves in like a ripe canta-loupe…Shalimar?

**SHALIMAR.** Yeah.

**THE DUDE.** It's your turn. Ready a spell!

(SHALIMAR's *been waiting for this. She gets up too. She re-wraps her feather boa and then kind of wiggles.*)

**SHALIMAR.** (*Singing Aretha:*) "R. E. S. P. E. C. T…tell me what it means to me—"

**D.M.** Hey! 'Tard! You wanna tell me what you're readying?

**SHALIMAR.** I'm preparing…a cone of SILENCE!

(THE DUDE *stops smiting.*)

**THE DUDE.** Christine. You had a cone of silence the whole time?

**SHALIMAR.** Yeah.

**THE DUDE.** (*To D.M.:*) She had a cone of silence the whole time.

**D.M.** She's a level three priestess. She should.

**THE DUDE.** Well. Fuck me.

(*Sitting down heavily:*)

I want a re-do.

**SHALIMAR.** (*Stopping the wiggling:*) Andrew. I can use any spell I want to. There's no rules about which spell I can use or can't use.

**THE DUDE.** (*To D.M.:*) Why do we always have to play with the 'tard?

**D.M.** Since Darryl moved to Jersey it's her or a one on one. And only fags play D&D one on one.

**SHALIMAR.** David. Can you tell—

(*As nasty as she can manage:*)

—The Dude. That I can cast any spell I want to.

**THE DUDE.** That's not the point. The point is…why the hell didn't you cast it before I went sneaking over by tent full of ruffians? I'm standing over there SMITING with my bare hands. It's a joke! Why would a brute force barbarian trek with a six-foot-two mulatto Amazon if she's got AMNESIA!?!

**D.M.** Easy on the 'tard, Drew. She has been your firm ally throughout the lost lands.

**THE DUDE.** *What*ever.

(*Through the door enters* BETH. *She's dressed like a 22-year-old should be dressed in 1985. She's Shalimar and D.M.'s older sister.*)

**BETH.** You guys wanna keep it down—

(*Eyes widen:*)

Oh God. What the hell?

*(They all freeze. Especially* THE DUDE. *He's mortified to be caught in his fur tunic. He quickly removes it and sits down.* SHALIMAR *unwraps her boa and sets it on the table.* D.M. *keeps his helmet on. Of the three he is the only one unaffected by Beth's presence.)*

Aren't we all a little too old to be playing Pebbles and Bam-bam?

**SHALIMAR.** I'm actually an Amazon.

**D.M.** Get out of the dungeon, Beth.

*(Forceful, but calm:)*

You wanna get out of my dungeon.

*(*BETH *steps over to* THE DUDE *and picks up his tunic.)*

**BETH.** What are you supposed to be Drew. Grizzly Adams?

**THE DUDE.** A barbarian.

**BETH.** A barbarian with braces?

**D.M.** His name is "The Dude." He bears the sign of the devil on his brow. He's the last monarch of Atlantis. And…I asked you before to get out of here.

**BETH.** It's my house too and I outrank you.

**D.M.** So hang out in the living room.

**BETH.** I can't smoke a joint in the living room.

*(That turns* THE DUDE's *head.)*

**THE DUDE.** You're going to smoke pot?

*(Off her nod:)*

Holy shit! Can I watch.

**BETH.** *(Sitting on the floor, twisting her J:)* Holee sheeet! Holee sheeet!

**D.M.** Just ignore her.

**THE DUDE.** But she's gonna roll a—

**D.M.** —And you're in the middle of a melee.

**SHALIMAR.** I'm casting a spell.

**D.M.** That's right. Shalimar is casting a spell. And THE DUDE is smiting the fierce barbarians…

**BETH.** *(Snickering:) The Dude.*

*(*D.M. *rolls the dice. And rolls them. And rolls them.* THE DUDE *turns to watch* BETH. *Then back to the dice.)*

**D.M.** The Dude. The last fierce warrior king sold into slavery by the Atlantean wizards. The Dude. Level 9 fighter. The Dude wields his fists like—

*(Beat.)*

—tell her, Dude.

*(*ANDREW *shakes his head. He can't.)*

**SHALIMAR.** He's got plus 2 fists.

**D.M.** *(Plaintive. It matters:)* Tell her Dude.

> *(BETH has finished rolling her joint. She looks up.)*

**THE DUDE.** My character has got uhh…magical gloves that make his fists as hard as…

> *(Her face makes it impossible.)*

…ah shit. Is that a real joint?

**BETH.** Does Frodo smoke pot?

**THE DUDE.** I've smoked pot before.

**BETH.** Oh. *Really?*

> *(D.M. is steaming under his helmet.)*

**D.M.** Dude. You gonna play or throw wood?

**THE DUDE.** Hold it a sec…

> *(To* BETH*:)*

I did smoke a joint before.

**D.M.** Dude?

**BETH.** Bravo. 'Drew has officially joined the ranks of the oregano smokers.

> *(To* SHALIMAR, *as she lights up:)*

Chrissy. You want some?

> *(SHALIMAR nods and goes to sit next to* BETH.*)*

**D.M.** Dude.

**THE DUDE.** *(Ignoring D.M.:)* It wasn't oregano.

> *(D.M. knocks his fist on the table. No results. He starts rolling the dice. He consults his pad.)*

*(Standing:)* It wasn't oregano. I was up on the hill with Jeff and Ray and two guys that were camping up there gave us a real joint—

> *(D.M. finishes rolling.)*

**D.M.** —and isn't that a lucky roll—

**THE DUDE.** —and I got stoned.

> *(BETH stands up, takes SHALIMAR's hand. With her joint cradled she heads for the door.)*

**BETH.** Whatever. *(Yawns.)* Family Ties is on in 5. Later zipper-head.

> *(D.M. looks up at THE DUDE. THE DUDE is pining. D.M. takes off his helmet. He's pissed. Really pissed.)*

**D.M.** Game over, Dude.

**THE DUDE.** *(Calls after* BETH*:)* —and we didn't giggle at all. We talked about cloud shapes…

*(Just hearing what* D.M. *said:)*
What?

**D.M.** You're dead, dude. You were too busy fucking around with my sisters. You died.

*(*THE DUDE's *attention towards* BETH *vanishes. He looks over at* D.M. *total panic washing over his face.)*

**THE DUDE.** Oh come on. That's impossible.

**D.M.** Serious. Look at the dice. The bug-bear got loose. Lucky bite. Took your head off.

**THE DUDE.** David. Don't be a fuck.

**D.M.** You're dead, Dude. *(Cruel:)* I mean…'Drew.

*(Total shock washes over* THE DUDE.*)*

**THE DUDE.** Shalimar can cast a resurrect.

**D.M.** Shalimar's only level 3.

**THE DUDE.** We can have a do-over.

*(*D.M. *shakes his head. "No we can't.")*

David. I've been playing as The Dude since we were fourteen. He can't die.

**D.M.** He just did.

*(*THE DUDE *pushes his chair back. Stands on it. Sits. Waves his arms.)*

**THE DUDE.** This game never happened.

**D.M.** Yes, it did.

*(*THE DUDE *stands up. He just can't believe it.)*

**THE DUDE.** That's bullshit.

*(*D.M. *puts on his helmet.)*

**D.M.** Wrong, I'm the Dungeon Master. This is my realm. I decide who lives and dies. I'm the Master of the World! From Mordor to the river Styx. You chose to hang with harpies instead of reclaiming your barbarian crown, well, then, if I say THE DUDE THE BARBARIAN is DEAD. Then he's history.

*(No way.* THE DUDE *takes his papers and walks to the door.)*

**THE DUDE.** Then get another best friend.

**D.M.** No problem.

*(*THE DUDE *turns back to* D.M. *All of a sudden he's a barbarian.)*

**THE DUDE.** You know what I'm going to do later?

**D.M.** Like I care.

**THE DUDE.** I'm going to go home and think about your sister's tits and jerk off.

*(Fade out.)*

## End of Play

# JACK ON FILM
## by Adam Rapp

## BIOGRAPHY

Adam Rapp is an award-winning novelist, playwright, director, and film-maker. He attended Clarke College in Dubuque, IA, and Juilliard's Playwriting Program. He lives in New York City.

## ACKNOWLEDGMENTS

*Jack on Film* was originally produced by The 24 Hour Company as a part of *The 24 Hour Plays on Broadway* at The American Airlines Theatre on October 23, 2006. It was directed by Ian Morgan with the following cast:

MAN A .................................................................. Sam Rockwell
MAN B .................................................................John Hawkes
MAN C .............................................................. Matthew Lillard
WOMAN.........................................................Erika Christensen

## CAST OF CHARACTERS

MAN A
MAN B
MAN C
WOMAN

# Jack on Film

*Two Men sitting in an early twentieth century English drawing room. They are both early thirties. MAN A is seated behind a desk. On the desk is a ten-page script, which he refers to now and then. It might appear as if he's reading from it at certain points. His feet are on the desk. MAN B is seated in the downstage sofa. They don't move very much. A short silence, then:*

**MAN B.** So this is pretty weird, right? I mean, the guy driving the van didn't say it was gonna be like this.

**MAN A.** Like what?

**MAN B.** Look at this place.

**MAN A.** What about it?

**MAN B.** The chandelier, the organ, the books so perfectly arranged in the bookcase. This sofa. The guy driving the van didn't say anything about it being… Well, it's like we're trapped in a fucking Shaw play or something.

**MAN A.** The guy driving the van didn't say anything.

**MAN B.** Before we got in the van he did. Before we got in the van he said that once we got to the house we were to find a comfortable spot to sit and not to move until we're called into the other room.

**MAN A.** But in the van he just drove.

**MAN B.** Maybe you're right.

**MAN A.** You also might have noticed he was wearing a black ski mask.

*(A pause.)*

**MAN B.** Why aren't we supposed to move? What's that about?

**MAN A.** I don't know. Keeps things simple, I guess.

**MAN B.** Simple, sure… But doesn't it freak you out a little?

**MAN A.** When someone hands me thousands of dollars and all I have to do is get in a van, go to some house in the country, and try not to move until I'm called in to another room to be interviewed on film, I'm not going to ask too many questions?

**MAN B.** They gave you thousands of dollars?

**MAN A.** Thousands, yep.

**MAN B.** How many thousands?

**MAN A.** Like in the upper nineties. Just kidding. Let's call it four and a half.

**MAN B.** Four and a half. I only got a grand.

**MAN A.** Life's a bitch and then you die.

*(MAN A crosses his legs on the desk. Or if they are already crossed, he recrosses them.)*

**MAN B.** Um, you just moved.

**MAN A.** I did. I did in fact just move. But not very much. Got any blow?

**MAN B.** Blow, no. I don't... Cocaine's not for me.

**MAN A.** Right on.

(*Pause.*)

**MAN B.** Hey, what's your name, anyway? I know we're probably not supposed to—

**MAN A.** Jack, what's yours?

**MAN B.** Um, Drrrave.

**MAN A.** Drave?

**MAN B.** Drave, yeah.

**MAN A.** Is that a name?

**MAN B.** I mean Jack. I'm Jack, too.

**MAN A.** Crazy.

**MAN B.** Really crazy.

**MAN A.** Two Jacks in the same room. The world is a glorious fucking card trick. Ask me my last name?

**MAN B.** What's your last name?

**MAN A.** Oft.

**MAN B.** Oft?

**MAN A.** Jack Oft, yep. What's yours?

**MAN B.** Katagas...saki. I mean North.

**MAN A.** Jack North.

**MAN B.** Jack P. North, yeah.

**MAN A.** You're nervous, aren't you.

**MAN B.** And you're not?

**MAN A.** Not really, no.

(*Pause.*)

**MAN B.** Hey, are you like reading from a script?

**MAN A.** This is a script, yes.

**MAN B.** What is it? I mean, if you don't mind me asking.

**MAN A.** It's the story of your life, Jack P. North. I'm going to change the subject, is that cool?

**MAN B.** Sure.

**MAN A.** Why'd you do it?

**MAN B.** Do what?

**MAN A.** Accept the money. Get in the van. Take the risk. Random guy walks up to you at the florist.

**MAN B.** It was in a parking garage, actually.

**MAN A.** Random guy walks up to you in a paring lot, offers you a grand to do some weird shit and you decide to get in a van.

**MAN B.** Well, I'm pretty strapped.

**MAN A.** Aren't we all.

**MAN B.** I haven't been bringing in too much money lately. And my daughter's sick. She has lupus and my insurance just ran out, and my wife sort of left us a few months ago, so…

**MAN A.** What do you do?

**MAN B.** I'm an actor.

**MAN A.** Oh. Wow, an actor. Dramarama. Would I have seen you in anything?

**MAN B.** No, prolly not. I do theatre mostly. That's why I—

**MAN A.** The Shaw comment, right.

**MAN B.** I was actually gonna say that's why I use the middle initial. Because in the union—it's called Actor's Equity Association—in the union two people can't have the same name.

**MAN A.** Jack P. North.

**MAN B.** That's me.

**MAN A.** What's the P stand for?

**MAN B.** It's just a P… Well, Paul, if you want to know the truth.

**MAN A.** Jack Paul North. Can you do accents?

**MAN B.** Sure.

**MAN A.** Do one.

**MAN B.** Like right now?

**MAN A.** Yeah, show me what you got. Gimme some Shaw.

**MAN B.** Okay… *(With British accent:)* "Have I done anything to annoy you, mother? If so, it was quite unintentional." That was Stephen from Major Barbara, Act I. Scene I.

**MAN A.** I'm fucking impressed.

**MAN B.** Thanks.

**MAN A.** Shaw would be proud, Jack.

**MAN B.** Thanks so much, man. What do you do? Are you an actor, too? I mean I only ask because of the script.

**MAN A.** I'm actually a cocaine addict. And I kill people.

**MAN B.** Oh.

> *(Pause.)*
> *(A sexual noise from off.)*

**MAN B.** Did you just hear that?

**MAN A.** What?

**MAN B.** That noise. It sounded…well, sexual.

**MAN A.** Didn't hear it.

(MAN B *looks back at* MAN A.)

**MAN A.** What.

**MAN B.** Nothing.

**MAN A.** You just looked at me funny.

**MAN B.** I did?

**MAN A.** I would qualify that as a funny look, North. What's on your mind?

**MAN B.** Do you think we look alike?

**MAN A.** I don't know. Do you?

**MAN B.** I'm not sure.

**MAN A.** Why do you ask?

**MAN B.** Because the guy who set this up. Not the guy in the van, the other guy.

**MAN A.** The guy with the hole in his face.

**MAN B.** Yeah, the guy with the hole in his face.

**MAN A.** The guy who walked up to you in the parking garage. The guy who gave you the money.

**MAN B.** Yeah, the guy who gave me the money. He told me that he was looking for three guys who looked alike.

**MAN A.** I think in a certain like we could possibly favor each other.

**MAN B.** Cool. I mean, you're a good looking guy is all, so that's cool.

**MAN A.** Are you hitting on me, Jack?

**MAN B.** No, I was just… No.

(*The door opens. Suddenly* MAN C *enters from the stage left French doors. He is wearing his underwear and carrying his clothes. He is filled with a kind of apocalyptic terror, but is also perhaps a bit stunned in what might be perceived to be in a coitally shocked sort of way. He eases into the room, stops.*)

**MAN C.** She said she's ready to see Jack.

**MAN B.** Which one?

**MAN C.** I don't know. She just said Jack.

**MAN A.** Go 'head.

**MAN B.** You think?

**MAN A.** Sure.

(MAN B *slowly stands.*)

**MAN B.** (*To* MAN C:) Is there anything I should know?

**MAN C.** Just make sure to say your lines right. And whatever you do, don't touch the camera.

**MAN B.** *(Confused:)* Okay… *(To* MAN C:*)* Are you all right?

**MAN C.** I'm better off than I was when I went in, I can tell you that much.

**MAN A.** *(To* MAN B:*)* You better get in there.

(MAN B *nods, crosses to the French doors, looks back once.)*

**MAN B.** *(To* MAN A:*)* Thanks for the conversation.

**MAN A.** Hey, good luck.

(MAN B *exits through the French doors.)*

(MAN C *takes Man B's spot on the sofa, starts to put his clothes on.)*

**MAN C.** So your name's Jack, too?

**MAN A.** It is. What's yours?

**MAN C.** Roy.

**MAN A.** Are you an actor, too?

**MAN C.** No, I'm a machinist. Work over at Morrison Brothers. What about you?

**MAN A.** I'm a cocaine addict.

**MAN C.** Seriously?

**MAN A.** In all seriousness, yes.

**MAN C.** But do you like have a job?

**MAN A.** I'm a careerist.

**MAN C.** A careerist. I gotta remember that one.

(Pause. MAN C *continues to get dressed.)*

**MAN C.** Man, that is one powerful woman in there. And she's got those eyes. Like a wildcat. To think I got paid five hundred bucks to do *that*. They paid *me*. Weird… So I guess you're next, huh?

**MAN A.** You got it.

**MAN C**. Hey, can I ask you a question?

**MAN A.** You just did. But double your luck.

**MAN C.** Double my luck, you're hilarious… Seriously, though, do you think that guy who just went in, do you think him and I look alike?

**MAN A.** I think you do, yeah.

**MAN C.** I sorta thought that when I came out… Strange coincidence, this whole thing. I mean, one day you're scraping rust off the bottom of your car, and then this guy shows up in your driveway and just starts talking to you. Wanna be in a movie? Make X amount of dollars. Life is crazy… So are you excited to go in?

**MAN A.** I can't even begin to tell you.

**MAN C.** You been preparing? You got like a plan and all?

**MAN A.** I do. I do, in fact, hava a plan.

**MAN C.** What is it?

**MAN A.** *(Producing a jump rope:)* Well, my plan is to wait for you to leave, and then when I get my cue, I'm going to use this jump rope to go strangle our friend Jack.

**MAN C.** You're kidding, right?

**MAN A.** I'm not kidding at all.

**MAN C.** *(Laughing:)* You're gonna strangle him.

**MAN A.** *(Laughing, too:)* I most certainly am, Roy.

**MAN C.** And then what?

**MAN A.** And then I plan on using the several thousand dollars that they're paying me to go find about a kilo of cocaine and lock myself in my amazing house and do as many lines as I possibly can while a rotisserie of beautiful women visit me.

> *(The sound of* MAN B *screaming from off. The screaming is muffled.)*

**MAN C.** You're serious, aren't you?

> *(*MAN A *doesn't answer. A weird silence.)*

**MAN C.** How do you get out of here, anyway? This place gives me the creeps.

> *(*MAN A *points to the thin stage right exit, just downstage of the desk.* MAN C, *dressed now, moves toward the exit, eases by* MAN A, *who is still loosely holding the jump rope.* MAN C *exits.)*
>
> *(Moments later, The French doors open and a* WOMAN *enters. She is wearing a robe and carrying a role of silver duct tape. She sits on the downstage sofa.* MAN A *crosses, joins her on the sofa.)*

**MAN A.** Everything all set?

**WOMAN.** Everything's all set. He kept talking about his daughter. Things got a little loud so I had to—

**MAN A.** Yeah, I heard… What are you shooting this on, anyway?

**WOMAN.** Mini DV.

**MAN A.** You got your gear all set up?

**WOMAN.** The shot's good. Just make sure you keep his legs away from the tripod.

**MAN A.** You're happy with the angle?

**WOMAN.** The angle's perfect.

**MAN A.** And you're sure you don't want to be in the room to see it?

**WOMAN.** It'll be better if I'm out here.

**MAN A.** Suit yourself. Is he afraid?

**WOMAN.** Very much, yes.

**MAN A.** Good… Camera's rolling?

**WOMAN.** *(Nodding:)* I think this is going to be a really important film.

> *(He stands, gently twists the ends of the jump rope around his fists. He bends down, kisses her on the mouth.)*

**MAN A.** The script is really good.

**WOMAN.** Thanks.

**MAN A.** I fucking love film jobs.

> *(She nods, touching his face.)*
>
> *(MAN A hands her the script, crosses to the French doors, exits. Moments later, we hear the muffled screams of MAN B. After a moment, nothing.)*
>
> *(The WOMAN weeps on the sofa.)*

## *End of Play*

# OPEN HOUSE
## by Theresa Rebeck

# BIOGRAPHY

Theresa Rebeck's past New York productions include *The Water's Edge*, *Spike Heels*, *Loose Knit* and *The Family of Mann* at Second Stage; *Bad Dates* and *The Butterfly Collection* at Playwrights Horizons; and *View of the Dome* at New York Theatre Workshop. *Omnium Gatherum* (co-written with Alexandra Gersten-Vassilaros, and finalist for the Pulitzer Prize) was featured at the Humana Festival 2003, and had a commercial run at the Variety Arts. Her play *The Scene*, produced at the Humana Festival in March of 2006, will be seen at Second Stage as part of the 2006-2007 season. Her work has been widely produced both regionally and internationally. She is currently working on commissions from Playwrights Horizons, Denver Theatre Center, and Cincinnati Playhouse in the Park.

In television, Ms. Rebeck has written for *Dream On*, *Brooklyn Bridge*, *L.A. Law*, *Maximum Bob*, *First Wave*, *Third Watch*, and *NYPD Blue*, where she also worked as a producer. Produced features include *Harriet the Spy*, *Gossip*, and the independent feature *Sunday on the Rocks*. Awards include the Mystery Writers of America's Edgar Award, the Writer's Guild of America award for Episodic Drama, the Hispanic Images Imagen Award, and the Peabody, all for her work on *NYPD Blue*. She has been a finalist for the Susan Smith Blackburn prize twice, won the National Theatre Conference Award (for *The Family of Mann*), and was awarded the William Inge New Voices Playwriting Award in 2003.

Ms. Rebeck holds a PhD. from Brandeis University in Victorian Melodrama. She and her husband Jess Lynn have two children, Cooper and Cleo.

## ACKNOWLEDGMENTS

*Open House* was originally produced by The 24 Hour Company at The American Airlines Theatre on the set of *Pygmalion* in New York City on October 22, 2007. It was directed by Ari Edelson with the following cast:

GABY ............................................................Gabrielle Hoffman
KRISTIN..........................................................Kirsten Johnston
JEREMY.....................................................................Jeremy Sisto
DIANE.................................................................... Diane Neal
CRAIG........................................................Craig "muMs" Grant

## CAST OF CHARACTERS

GABY
KRISTIN
JEREMY
DIANE
CRAIG

# OPEN HOUSE

GABY *and* KRISTIN *standing in a lovely, if small, Victorian study.* GABY *looks around.* KRISTIN *watches her, nervous.*

**KRISTIN.** So…what do you think?

**GABY.** What do I think? It's…pretty…fucking…Park Slope, is what I think.

**KRISTIN.** I like it. And, they think it's going to move.

**GABY.** Move? The house is going to move? That I would like to see.

**KRISTIN.** You don't like it.

**GABY.** I didn't say that.

**KRISTIN.** Oh my god.

**GABY.** I did not say I didn't like it! I said that given that it's Park Slope it doesn't make me wretch.

**KRISTIN.** There's a ringing endorsement.

**GABY.** What do you want me to say.

**KRISTIN.** What is wrong with Park Slope. It's pretty.

**GABY.** Pretty, absolutely it's pretty. It's fucking adorable.

**KRISTIN.** *(Getting tense:)* I like it here. I like the block and I like the trees and the restaurants and the bookstores and and and you know the house is, I love this house. The woodwork. And the wall paper. The bedrooms and the moldings and the the parlor floor is so pretty.

**GABY.** Pretty, apparently, is a big word today.

**KRISTIN.** *(Snapping:)* Okay what is wrong with "pretty"?

**GABY.** Nothing is wrong with pretty. This whole place is completely pretty; it's total Victorianorama. It's like "Park Slope." "Park Slope"!

**KRISTIN.** It is Park Slope!

**GABY.** Oh look, Volvos! Oh look, baby strollers! Oh look, movie stars!

**KRISTIN.** You love movie stars. We lived in Los Angeles, all you ever wanted to do was go to the Chateau Marmont for drinks. That was all you ever—

**GABY.** They had really good martinis there. And the ambiance was fantastic.

**KRISTIN.** They had shitty martinis and the ambiance was shit!

**GABY.** You told me sixteen thousand times you loved it. Old Hollywood. The glamour. The decadence.

**KRISTIN.** Four floors. Plus a cellar.

**GABY.** This isn't a floor, this is an attic!

**KRISTIN.** Who cares! The parlor floor is bigger than the entire state of Rhode Island! And it's under two point five. In New York.

**GABY.** Give me a break.

**KRISTIN.** Two point five, in New York!

**GABY.** It's BROOKLYN.

> *(JEREMY enters. He looks around.)*

**JEREMY.** Hey.

**KRISTIN.** Hey.

**JEREMY.** This place is nice, huh.

**KRISTIN.** Wonderful.

> *(He looks around. GABY stews. KRISTIN smiles at him, polite. A beat as he looks around, then:)*

**JEREMY.** These old houses. Fantastic, right? You see that painting in the bathroom?

**KRISTIN.** Uh—no.

**JEREMY.** Oh yeah, the third floor bathroom, it has like this painting on the wall, behind the shower? Those little fat babies with wings, and this dude pushing a girl on a swing. No shit. It's like this huge, right on the wall, I missed it at first because it was behind the shower curtain but it is completely—well, it's pretty ugly honestly, is what I thought, like what the fuck were they thinking? Painting that shit on the bathroom wall? You got to ask yourself. And you're like stuck with it obviously because it's totally historically you just wouldn't mess with something like that. But this is nice. Wow. This is like awesome. And how much are they asking for the whole place, two point five?

**KRISTIN.** *(Pointed:)* Yes! Two point five!

**GABY.** And what's on the wall of the bathroom? A girl on a swing and little fat flying babies?

**JEREMY.** You could probably cover it up with a shower curtain or something.

**GABY.** Yeah but for two point five do you really want to do that?

**JEREMY.** I don't know. The garden's pretty nice. Like in Manhattan? Four floors plus a garden? That would be like twenty million dollars or something.

**KRISTIN.** Plus a cellar. A finished cellar.

**JEREMY.** Right? Still, it is Brooklyn. You live in New York you go, do you really want to live in Brooklyn? You may as well live in Ohio, or something.

**GABY.** Yes.

**JEREMY.** So you gonna make an offer? Just kidding. Not. Seriously, you think it'll move?

**KRISTIN.** I couldn't say.

**JEREMY.** No no. Of course. Sorry. Didn't mean to, you know. It's just nerve wracking. Real estate. Like you don't want to keep renting that is just like so fucking obvious you run the numbers even like once even you're kind of a moron about math, it's totally clear renting is for losers. But like a whole house. In Brooklyn? That's the sort of thing like the next thing you know you're staring at some cadaver version of yourself in the mirror wondering why you put up with a boss who's just a total dick for thirty years, or or or did you really marry the right person or did you just get talked into it in a kind of boneheaded way OR like suddenly you're a fat fuck drinking beer and moaning about the Mets and you never went to India or Mexico or even like a pub crawl in Europe, you never did any of that stuff because you worried you just worried all the time, about bullshit because everybody just kept telling you that you better get a clue and maybe maybe buy a house in Brooklyn with like a stupid picture of a girl on a swing, painted on the wall of your bathroom. Like that.

> *(Beat.)*

You should check that picture out, it's kind of interesting.

**KRISTIN.** Thanks we'll do that.

**JEREMY.** Yeah.

> *(He goes.* GABY *rolls her eyes at* KRISTIN. *There is a pause.)*

**GABY.** Well. I think my point has been made.

**KRISTIN.** I don't. Why? Because some sad loser walked in and said insane things for two minutes? Welcome to New York.

**GABY.** We are not making an offer on this house.

**KRISTIN.** It's under two point five.

**GABY.** We're not doing it.

**KRISTIN.** It's beautiful. It's gorgeous. It would be like living in an Edith Wharton novel.

**GABY.** There's a life's dream.

**KRISTIN.** We're six blocks from ten different subway lines!

**GABY.** Lesbians in Park Slope. That's what you want.

**KRISTIN.** Park Slope is a perfectly decent place to be a lesbian!

**GABY.** Yeah, sure, sure. Why don't you just write a memoir, while you're at it. You know what else we could do? We could adopt a baby! From China!

**KRISTIN.** We are not making an offer on that place in the East Village. It is half this size, the plumbing is for shit and there are RATS and HEROIN ADDICTS.

**GABY.** That guy was not a heroin addict. He was diabetic.

**KRISTIN.** He was not!

**GABY.** You want to be a lesbian in Park Slope. That's what you want out of life, that's what you want.

**KRISTIN.** What the fuck, are you kidding me? What the fuck do you want?

*(The door opens and* DIANE *comes in.)*

**DIANE.** Hi, excuse me hi—am I interrupting? I hope I'm not interrupting.

**GABY.** Not at all.

**DIANE.** All those stairs. I'm just bushed. Well this is charming! Isn't this charming! Mark come see how charming this is! We'll be right out of your hair in just two little seconds. Mark honey! It's a real cute room! Isn't this cute. Do these drawers work? Oh it might be rude to look. Do you think it's rude to look in other people's closets and such?

**GABY.** I do actually yes I would consider it the height of rudeness if I found out that total strangers were looking through my drawers.

**DIANE.** Well I just wanted to see if they work.

**GABY.** Nevertheless.

**DIANE.** It is an open house.

**GABY.** Listen you asked my opinion I gave it to you

**KRISTIN.** *(Impatient, finally:)* I'm sure it would be fine if you wanted to open a drawer or two.

**GABY.** *(Sharp:)* I don't think it would be fine. In some places it might be fine? But in this place I am fairly certain it would not be fine.

**DIANE.** Oh well it was just a thought.

**KRISTIN.** It's an open house. Why would you come to the house and not look at the house.

**GABY.** I didn't say you wouldn't look at the house. I said some places don't invite you in. Some places don't say, come on in, open the drawers, see how you would fit here—

**KRISTIN.** That's ridiculous.

**DIANE.** We could just ask.

**GABY.** Or no no no , some places say, go ahead and look? But if you do what you will find is an ugly painting on the wall of fat flying babies, and memories of what a good time you had in Hollywood, and how even living with rats and drug addicts would be better than sucking it up with a lot of fucking STROLLERS and VOLVOS and MOVIE STARS and LESBIANS.

*(A terrible pause.)*

**DIANE.** You know what? The real estate agent was just downstairs on the third floor landing! I'm just going to go ask him, okay?

*(She goes.* KRISTIN *shakes her head, looks around.)*

**KRISTIN.** There is nothing wrong with this house.

**GABY.** Everything is wrong with this house.

**KRISTIN.** I like it here. I don't think baby strollers are some hideous offense against humanity. I like book stores. I like trees. I like the word pretty.

**GABY.** You like Volvos.

**KRISTIN.** I don't like Volvos. But I don't want to live with heroin addicts. And I don't think that makes me…old.

**GABY.** He was a diabetic.

*(There is a sad pause, and* CRAIG *enters.)*

**CRAIG.** *(Bright:)* Hello, hello, how are we doing up here? It's a fantastic house, isn't it, just a dream of a house! This house is not going to be on the market for long I assure you. There is a lot of love here not to mention complete value for your dollar. You had a question about the drawers I think, and I can tell you that they work perfectly well but for now I am going to ask you NOT to open the drawers, the owners have some personal items stored in there so for now, no drawers will be opened. But other than that, did you find everything you were looking for?

**KRISTIN.** Yes I think we did.

**GABY.** We did, yes. We did.

*(*KRISTIN *and* GABY *stare at each other. Blackout.)*

## *End of Play*

# I'M ALL ABOUT LESBIANS
## by Mac Rogers

## BIOGRAPHY

Mac Rogers is a playwright and performer who lives in Brooklyn with his fiancé Sandy. Playscripts, Inc. previously published his play *The Second String*. His play *Universal Robots* was anthologized in the New York Theatre Experience's "Plays and Playwrights 2008" anthology, and *Hail Satan* won a Fringe-NYC 2007 Outstanding Playwriting Award. Along with Sean and Jordana Williams, Mac wrote *Fleet Week: The Musical*, winner of a FringeNYC 2005 Outstanding Musical Award. Mac's other plays produced in New York include *Dirty Juanita, The Sky Over Nineveh*, and *The Lucretia Jones Mysteries*. As an actor, Mac was nominated for a New York Innovative Theater Award for his performance in Nosedive Productions' *The Adventures of Nervous Boy*.

## ACKNOWLEDGMENTS

*I'm All About Lesbians* was originally produced by The 24 Hour Company at the Ohio Theatre in New York City in February 2000. It was directed by Moh Azima with the following cast:

PINNIX.................................................................... John Connolly
MADDY............................................................Susan Mitchell
HANNAH...................................................... Sarah Rubenstein
PIPER ........................................................ Gwendolyn Chavez

## CAST OF CHARACTERS

PINNIX, male, younger
MADDY, female, older
HANNAH, female, younger
PIPER, in the middle

# I'M ALL ABOUT LESBIANS

*The characters are always onstage, seated in chairs. They get up and come forward when they are involved in the action. If desired, this can be done in the manner of a radio play, everybody at stands with papers on them.*

*Lights up on* PINNIX.

**PINNIX.** My name is Pinnix, and I'm all about lesbians. Lesbians are what I'm about. Lesbians are the air I breathe, the sun that shines on me, my food, my drink, my needle, my powder, my first cigarette in the morning and the last one before I go to sleep at night. I love me some lesbians.

*(Enter* MADDY, *reading a copy of Maxim with Lara Flynn Boyle on the cover.)*

Here's one now.

**MADDY.** Hi.

**PINNIX.** Maddy Cardinal. She's a lesbian.

*(She shrugs at us, and returns to the magazine.)*

She likes girls. I do too, mind you, but it's problematic. I like girls in the abstract. I like them in a pageant, you know, arranged. A configuration. Like, for example: "Bunny" is here, splayed back, eyes closed, on account of the gallant and arduous service being provided for her by "Amber." I don't want to meet Bunny, you understand, and I don't want to meet Amber, but I want to place them. I want to lock them around each other, and then step back and admire my handiwork. I don't want to talk to them. If I want to talk to a woman, I'll talk to Maddy. *(Pause.)* I mean, I understand your reaction. There's no doubt I have emotional problems.

**MADDY.** *(Holding up the magazine:)* Lara Flynn Boyle.

**PINNIX.** Is it?

**MADDY.** From TV's "The Practice."

**PINNIX.** Oh yeah—Golden Globes and stuff.

*(*MADDY *flips open to the front page of the Lara Flynn Boyle spread; she's been holding her place.)*

**MADDY.** "Verdict: Hot."

**PINNIX.** She's alright.

**MADDY.** No, I'm serious.

**PINNIX.** She could eat. I mean, I'm the worst class of pig, but she could seriously have a bowl of soup or something.

**MADDY.** No, that's not me, Pinnix, that's the geniuses at Maxim: "Verdict" —colon—"Hot." You know, on account of her being on a court show.

**PINNIX.** Awesome.

**MADDY.** Revisionist-feminism, revisionist-revisionist feminism, post-feminism, fuck it: this is a magazine I could get behind. "Verdict: Hot." It's almost satire of the most eloquent pedigree. "Miss Flynn-Boyle, this court finds you guilty of being HOT!" *(She goes back to the cover.)* One alabaster buttcheek peering out like a crescent moon. Oh look: "Say, Are Those Briefs LEGAL?"

**PINNIX.** You like 'em?

**MADDY.** Only until I imagine Jack Nicholson removing them with his teeth.

**PINNIX.** You like 'em?

**MADDY.** Never leave me, Aaron. *(She sets the magazine down and returns to her chair.)*

**PINNIX.** Nobody else calls me Aaron, only Maddy. Otherwise, it's Pinnix. When your last name is "Pinnix," you can pretty much expect to be in private school for the rest of your life: you're always "Pinnix."

*(Towards the end of this,* HANNAH *gets up and goes to* PINNIX, *timing it out with him finishing.)*

**HANNAH.** Pinnix?

**PINNIX.** *(To us:)* Pinnix.

**HANNAH.** Pinnix.

**PINNIX.** This is Hannah.

*(*HANNAH *acknowledges us impatiently, and turns us back to* PINNIX.*)*

**HANNAH.** Can I send you out?

**PINNIX.** Boy, you're gonna have to narrow that down.

**HANNAH.** I need about a thousand things.

**PINNIX.** Oh, for the dinner. Groceries.

**HANNAH.** Yeah.

**PINNIX.** You already came home with like a billion things—

**HANNAH.** I need an additional thousand.

**PINNIX.** Duuuuuuuude…

**HANNAH.** Look, I'll make sexy faces later or something. What do you want?

**PINNIX.** I'm in the mood for Catwoman-type stuff. Pursed lips, a hint of danger—

**HANNAH.** Whatever.

**PINNIX.** Do one for me now?

**HANNAH.** Are you serious?

*(PINNIX shrugs. HANNAH is initially exasperated, but then she contorts her face into a comic-booky mask of sexual heat. Then she drops it.)*

Okay?

**PINNIX.** *(Relenting:)* Presumably you have a list.

*(She produces it instantly.)*

Sherbet, huh? I haven't had sherbet for a long time.

**HANNAH.** Well, there'll be like a kid's table or something, okay?

**PINNIX.** Hey, look, as long as I get the sherbet and the sexy faces, you do whatever you want. Your dime. *(Pause.)* Are you alright?

**HANNAH.** How old do you think I am?

**PINNIX.** Hannah, I went through your stuff. I know exactly how old you are. You turn twenty-seven in March. I'm not getting you a present.

**HANNAH.** I married Eric when I was twenty.

**PINNIX.** You had Sean when you were twenty-one and Adrian when you were twenty-two. But you went back to school three years later, nonetheless, over your husband's objections, and in your third semester you signed up for "Women's Empowerment Through Erotica" and here you are. I don't mean to be like this, I actually like you, but I keep stats on every one of you. I know everything.

**HANNAH.** There isn't going to be "every one of you" anymore.

**PINNIX.** Okay.

**HANNAH.** I'm making sure.

**PINNIX.** Okay.

**HANNAH.** I'm not going back. I have a stupid husband and two deafening children, all three of whom love me more than anything, and I'm not going back to them. That's what this is about. I'm with the most incredible woman I've ever known, and I'm going to be the one she can't do without.

**PINNIX.** And what with her ex coming over—

**HANNAH.** Exactly. It's the same skills, different pronoun. She'll be across the table from me—what's her name again?

**PINNIX.** Piper.

**HANNAH.** Piper?

**PINNIX.** Piper. You know. It beats Pinnix.

**HANNAH.** Alright: Piper. So Piper's across the table from me, and I'll be polite as you can imagine, but all the while, the vacuumed rugs, the mopped floors, the smell of the casserole, the bowls of sherbet—she'll hear loud and clear: "You didn't do this for her, did you, bitch? 'Piper?' You couldn't make her this food or give her this home. Was radical feminist theory alphabetized by author and/or editor when you were shacked up here? Bitch? What's that?

You don't remember? Well, I remember, SCAB, cause I alphabetized 'em! And if I can alphabetize that good, imagine how I can—you know—"

**PINNIX.** I'm imagining it right now.

**HANNAH.** *(Sudden, drastic mood swing:)* Just get me the stuff; I'm going insane.

**PINNIX.** *(He cools it:)* Okay. Okay.

    *(*HANNAH *returns to her seat.)*

D'Agostino, a loooong ice cream aisle. A loooong sherbet sub-section. You wouldn't think so, but normally, you really wouldn't think about sherbet.

I've never done a food run for run for any of Maddy's broads; Hannah's her first real domestic-type. I tell Maddy I cast her as the bored housewife, desperately unsatisfied by her brutish husband, sitting on the sun porch all day long dreaming of that soft, Sapphic touch that would set her free. I'd put her in an apron tied off in the back so you can undo it by pulling one loose end reeeeeeeeeeeeeal…slooooooooooooow… You know?

**MADDY.** *(From her chair:)* Don't ever leave me, Aaron.

**PINNIX.** I've cohabited with Maddy for three years now. I'm never leaving school, let's be honest, I'm gonna be one of those people who stays until they hire me out of exasperation. Mainly what I'm gonna do is look after Maddy. I'm her caretaker. I'm convinced I'm the only one who understands her.

**MADDY.** Aaron, you're the most gorgeously fucked-up human being I've ever known. It's like you're my creation. You're the pornographic sonnet I always used to tell people I would write. My own body-servant, spun out of the air. The unmanned man. Perfect.

**PINNIX.** I don't want the male body involved in the pageant. I'm consistent too—not even mine. I must have tried every kind of spank-mag amateur download in the Western World before I discovered "Spanish Eyes," the first installment in Maddy's "Touch" series. I applied to this school just to be near her. I'm her editor. I'm her sounding-board. I'm her archivist. I'm her companion. I'm the guy who's *there*. *There* is where I want to be. I'm all about lesbians.

    *(*PIPER *rises and takes a position in the center of the stage: immovable, a rock.* HANAH *and* MADDY *join us at the front.* PIPER *never speaks. The other characters speak to her and react to her, but* PINNIX *does the talking for her.)*

**HANNAH.** Piper showed up at eight-thirty and for close to one hour now she's behaved perfectly. She likes the casserole, she likes the string beans, she likes the salad, she likes the wine. She distributes the eye contact: she starts a sentence looking at Maddy, she looks at me in the middle, and then back to Maddy for the finish. It's just courtesy, but the effort is just so cool! I didn't figure her for it!

**MADDY.** *(To* HANNAH:*)* She's strange. She doesn't want to reminisce. She doesn't want to tell old stories or hear about them. We keep steering away. Right now we're talking about mud-slides in Venezuela. Why are we talking about mudslides in Venezuela?

**HANNAH.** Maddy, how many nightmare scenarios haven't happened yet? Relax, alright? We're closing in on the sherbet! One last hump!

**PINNIX.** Piper's purpose is kind of unclear, although Maddy suspects she's here as an emissary to talk about a fellowship some of the riot-grrls on the faculty want to set up, because it helps to be able to walk into a faculty meeting with Maddy Cardinal's "yea" notched on your belt, even though Maddy will almost certainly not show up.

**MADDY.** I'm sure that's why she's here. There's no other reason.

**PINNIX.** Which is what makes it all the more astonishing when Hannah says—

**HANNAH.** Two kids, the height of energy and need, it was just survival before that—what Maddy helped me discover in that class was the greatest revelation of my life.

**PINNIX.** —and Piper says, "I know what you mean. That's what I've found with the Lord Jesus Christ."

*(Pause.)*

**MADDY.** Say again?

**PINNIX.** *(To us:)* See, people should know, bring up the Lord Jesus Christ at dinner—it's just bad table manners.

**MADDY.** Piper, say what you just said again.

**PINNIX.** "Of course," says Piper, "that's why I'm here. This is what I came to say. These have been extraordinary months for me. I've discovered the most important thing in my life. I've discovered God's love."

**HANNAH.** *(To us:)* The air is turning toxic—some kind of mercury's falling somewhere.

**MADDY.** You have got to be kidding me. *(Pause.)* You're kidding me.

**PINNIX.** But no, she's not. Piper's wound all the way up and it's time to spring. The long months after Maddy tossed her out, back to her dissertation, back to the long sought-after PhD—and drinking, too. And pills. The whole hackneyed grad student smorgasbord. And nothing filled the hole. Nights got longer and longer, until one day—

**MADDY.** I don't want to hear it.

**PINNIX.** Until one day—

**MADDY.** I think you want to shut up, now.

**PINNIX.** Until one day a man stopped her on campus—and he was SO kind—

**MADDY.** Piper, you've had your tongue in my fucking cunt. I'd be very careful what you say next.

**PINNIX.** "He said, have you read the Gospels? Have you read the word of God?"

**MADDY.** I'm watching your face for any indication that this is unreal.

**HANNAH.** Maddy—

**MADDY.** I want to know this is a joke, or a dream—

**PINNIX.** "No joke," she says. "No joke. All those books, Maddy. Literature and criticism of the literature and criticism of the criticism—hasn't it ever gone cold for you? Hasn't it ever blurred before your eyes and turned to nonsense? There is an alternative."

**MADDY.** Were we sinners, Piper?

**PINNIX.** *(To us:)* Piper lasted eight months here. No one lasts eight months, but Piper did.

**MADDY.** What we had—look at me now—was that a sin?

**PINNIX.** And Piper says: "Love the sinner—hate the sin."

*(Pause. No one can think what to say.)*

"Love the sinner—hate the sin."

**HANNAH.** I think you should leave, now.

**PINNIX.** As bold as thunder, Piper turns on Hannah. "Do you miss your babies?"

**HANNAH.** What?

**PINNIX.** "Do you miss your babies, Hannah?"

**HANNAH.** ...do I miss them crying, screaming, running around, waking me up in the middle of the night, hitting, scratching each other, scratching me?

**PINNIX.** "Exactly," says Piper. "Those things. Do you miss them?"

*(She's got her. HANNAH may even cry.)*

**MADDY.** Get out. No. Get out. That fork in your hand—put it down and get out.

**PINNIX.** But Piper's not giving up: "Maddy, God's grace, I came here—

**MADDY.** *(Overlapping:)* God's grace, God's grace, get out of my house. You were a writer! Not a good one, but honest!

**PINNIX.** One last try: "Maddy! I came here for you! God's love—"

**MADDY.** I'll get a knife and stab you in the heart. Leave your plate, get out of that chair, get your coat, and go.

*(Pause. PIPER returns to her chair.)*

**PINNIX.** Piper never got to the sherbet. More for me, I guess. I mean, she's got God, I should get the sherbet.

(MADDY *is looking at* HANNAH.)

**MADDY.** What's wrong with you?

**HANNAH.** I'm sorry.

**MADDY.** Sean and Adrian.

**HANNAH.** Brats.

**MADDY.** You grew up in which faith? Remind me?

**HANNAH.** I've forgotten that now.

**MADDY.** Oh, I see. *(Pause.)* God's grace, Aaron?

**PINNIX.** Two women.

**MADDY.** God's grace is—?

**PINNIX.** The look on her face the first time she feels another woman's touch and everything changes.

**MADDY.** I wish I were you, Pinnix.

**PINNIX.** It's great to be me, Maddy.

**MADDY.** Hannah… *(She picks up the Maxim and holds it aloft.)* What would you do if you had Lara Flynn Boyle in your house?

(HANNAH *looks at the picture.*)

**HANNAH.** Feed her something.

**MADDY.** There. God's grace, see? "Whatever you do to be the least of these…" *(Pause.)* You have to go home.

**HANNAH.** What?

**MADDY.** Do you know why you're with me?

**HANNAH.** Because I love you.

**MADDY.** No, really.

**HANNAH.** What? Yes, really.

**MADDY.** It's been nice having you around.

**HANNAH.** What are you talking about?

**MADDY.** Warm body in the bed and everything, but now it's time for you to go.

*(Pause.)*

**HANNAH.** I left my children.

**MADDY.** Uh-huh. I'll call you a cab.

**PINNIX.** On it.

**HANNAH.** No, no, Pinnix—

**PINNIX.** The car service people?

**MADDY.** That's right.

**HANNAH.** I LEFT MY CHILDREN FOR YOU!

**MADDY.** Well, now you can go back. You're not bawling on my pillow tonight.

**HANNAH.** I can't…

**MADDY.** You'll find that you can. You can do just about anything.

(MADDY *leans over and kisses* HANAH. *The kiss freezes.*)

**PINNIX.** Two women kiss—man: it's a lot better reading about it. Even better is imagining it. Like they're doing it for me, they wouldn't be doing it, but for me. Broad A is here, Broad B slides in here. This shit, this shit here— *(He points at the frozen kiss.)* —this is two real people. This shit does nothing for me at all.

(*The kiss breaks.* HANNAH *returns to her chair.*)

**PINNIX.** Maddy and I have done this night so many times. After one of them goes. We've got it down to steps—me and her in the living room, just silent—she doesn't want me to do anything but sit there, and I can do that. I can do it all night if she wants. Then, when the cue triggers in her head:

**MADDY.** Never leave me, Aaron.

**PINNIX.** Never.

**MADDY.** Sometimes I think you'll leave me.

**PINNIX.** Never. You're the cat's pajamas.

**MADDY.** Aaron.

**PINNIX.** I think the sun shines out of you. I think without you plants wouldn't grow and man and beast wouldn't feed. Everything that sustains me comes from you.

**MADDY.** Girl-on-girl action.

**PINNIX.** You got that right. *(Pause.)*

**MADDY.** I'm going to watch television.

**PINNIX.** Alright.

(MADDY *returns to her chair.* PINNIX *speaks to us.*)

I'll go to bed first, but I won't sleep until I hear her door close. Then I'll select from my shelf of close to three hundred anthologies, looking for the novelty, the one I've forgotten, the one that's least stale from overuse and time. Then I'll use it, I'll clean up, I'll put it back where it was, and I'll go to sleep.

"X" marks the spot. She's where I'm always going to be. I'm Aaron Pinnix. And I'm all about lesbians.

(*Curtain.*)

## End of Play

# TWO WORLDS
## by Christopher Shinn

# BIOGRAPHY

Christopher Shinn was born in Hartford, Connecticut, and lives in New York. His plays have been premiered by the Royal Court, Lincoln Center, Manhattan Theatre Club, Playwrights Horizons, the Vineyard Theatre, South Coast Rep, and Soho Theatre, and later seen around the world. He is a winner of an OBIE in Playwriting, and a Guggenheim Fellowship in Playwriting. He has received grants from the NEA/TCG Residency Program and the Peter S. Reed Foundation, and he is recipient of the Robert S. Chesley Award. He teaches playwriting at the New School for Drama.

# ACKNOWLEDGMENTS

*Two Worlds* was originally produced by The 24 Hour Company at The Minetta Lane Theater in New York City on September 9, 2002. It was directed by Nela Wagman with the following cast:

FRED ........................................................................ Frank Wood
CARLA ................................................................. Drena DeNiro
NINA ........................................................................ Lili Taylor
TYLER ................................................................. Billy Crudup

# CAST OF CHARACTERS

FRED
CARLA
NINA
TYLER

# TWO WORLDS

*Two tables in a quiet restaurant. Classical music plays softly.*
*At one table,* CARLA *and* FRED *sit. At another table,* TYLER *sits quietly.*

**FRED.** Which, the thing is, is that sometimes you have to stay in the office till eight or nine. You know, because anything can happen. So they serve us dinner at the office, to encourage us not to leave the office. If we do go out, you know, we have our cell phones and our pagers and…you know, because anything can happen at any time. That's the nature of hedge funds. Markets…all around the world, everything affects everything.

**CARLA.** Right. How…fascinating.

**FRED.** I like numbers, what can I say. Numbers give me comfort, you know? Numbers…

**CARLA.** Uh-huh…

**FRED.** I mean, you know…

**CARLA.** I wonder where the waiter is. Speaking of numbers—we should probably get the check.

**FRED.** Oh. Right.

*(CARLA and FRED look around for the waiter. Behind TYLER, NINA appears. She looks at TYLER apprehensively.)*

**FRED.** I'll go find him.

*(FRED goes off to look for the waiter. NINA moves towards TYLER.)*

**NINA.** Tyler.

**TYLER.** *(Turning:)* Nina. Wow. My God.

*(A beat. NINA sits.)*

**NINA.** Hi.

**TYLER.** God. You look good.

**NINA.** Thank you.

**TYLER.** You're welcome.

*(A bit of an awkward pause.)*

**NINA.** Sorry I'm late.

**TYLER.** No, no…

**NINA.** Have you decided what you're getting or?…

**TYLER.** No…not yet.

**NINA.** Let's see what they have.

*(NINA looks at the menu on the table.* TYLER *follows.* FRED *returns to* CARLA.*)*

**FRED.** Hey there.

**CARLA.** Oh. Did you find the waiter?

**FRED.** I did.

**CARLA.** He's getting the check?

**FRED.** Well. Actually.

**CARLA.** Oh no.

**FRED.** I'm afraid the waiter talked me into dessert.

**CARLA.** Oh.

**FRED.** Strawberry bread pudding with fresh whipped cream.

**CARLA.** Oh. It's too bad I'm lactose intolerant.

**FRED.** Are you?

**CARLA.** Maybe there's time to cancel it.

**FRED.** I'll eat the whipped cream…you can still have the bread pudding, right?

**CARLA.** Sounds a little heavy…

**FRED.** Mm. Just a bite or two.

**CARLA.** Right…a bite or two…

> *(*CARLA *smiles and looks around the restaurant, as does* FRED. NINA *looks up from the menu.)*

**NINA.** I know what I'm going to have.

**TYLER.** Let me guess: grilled chicken Caesar salad.

**NINA.** No.

**TYLER.** No?

**NINA.** Oh, okay, yes.

**TYLER.** Ah-ha! I think I'll have…

**NINA.** A burger, swiss cheese, medium.

**TYLER.** Very good. Medium rare actually.

**NINA.** Living dangerously.

**TYLER.** On the edge. *(Pause.)* I miss you.

> *(NINA doesn't respond.)*

**TYLER.** How long has it been?

**NINA.** Months.

**TYLER.** Many. Months.

**NINA.** Yeah.

**TYLER.** I've really missed you.

**NINA.** And…

**TYLER.** And?

**NINA.** Is that it?

**TYLER.** Is what it?

**NINA.** All these months. And…you've missed me?

**TYLER.** Like I said.

(NINA *looks back down at the menu.* TYLER *looks at her a bit quizzically.*)

(CARLA *is still looking around the restaurant.*)

**FRED.** Somewhere to be?

**CARLA.** Oh…now that you ask…

**FRED.** Where?

**CARLA.** Oh, you know.

**FRED.** Right.

**CARLA.** Probably takes a little time to make a strawberry bread pudding. Not…not a "ready-made" dessert.

**FRED.** I'd suspect not.

**CARLA.** Probably kind of time-consuming.

**FRED.** Good things come to those who wait.

**CARLA.** Right.

(CARLA *looks around the restaurant.*)

**FRED.** I guess I'm not very good company.

**CARLA.** Oh…no, no. You're…you're…

**FRED.** I shouldn't even be on a date. I thought it would take my mind off things. But I can't get my mind off… I shouldn't even be talking about this but…have you ever seen anyone die?

(NINA *hears this and eavesdrops a little.*)

**CARLA.** Excuse me?

**FRED.** As I was walking here, looking at all the people on the street, I thought…everyone dies, each one of these people will die and…well… you've been on this earth a fair amount of time…you would think, in all your years, you might have seen someone die, so…just out of curiosity really… have you ever seen anyone die?

**CARLA.** No.

**FRED.** Me neither. Till a few months ago. And it's been…I guess it's been…sort of preoccupying me. Not exactly something you talk about on a first date. Oh, I better stop before I…you know what, I'll just get the check.

(FRED *goes, off.* CARLA *gets her things together.*)

**TYLER.** I'm sorry I caused you pain, Nina.

(NINA *looks to* TYLER.)

**TYLER.** I never meant to cause you pain.

**NINA.** But, you did.

**TYLER.** I did. And I'm sorry.

**NINA.** Right.

**TYLER.** I'm sorry I caused you pain.

**NINA.** Right.

**TYLER.** What?

**NINA.** No, just…

**TYLER.** No, just what?

**NINA.** You're sorry you caused me pain. After all these months…

**TYLER.** Yeah?

**NINA.** And I believe you. I believe you are sorry you caused me pain.

**TYLER.** And…I felt pain too. I feel pain. I want you back, Nina. I miss you so much.

**NINA.** You want me back.

**TYLER.** I do.

**NINA.** You miss me.

**TYLER.** Terribly.

**NINA.** I guess I just have one question.

**TYLER.** Yes.

**NINA.** What.

**TYLER.** The answer is yes.

**NINA.** What's the question?

**TYLER.** Isn't it…"Do you love me?" Do I love you, and the answer is yes, I do.

**NINA.** That isn't the question.

**TYLER.** Oh. Grilled chicken Caesar salad but not, "Do you love me?"

**NINA.** Do you know the question? Can you think of what I might be wanting an answer to?

*(Pause. TYLER thinks. FRED returns with the check, sits.)*

**CARLA.** Ah, the check.

**FRED.** I'll get it.

**CARLA.** No.

**FRED.** I insist.

*(FRED takes out his wallet.)*

Numbers. They're everywhere. You know why I love them so much?

**CARLA.** I can't begin to imagine.

**FRED.** They can change. Not like people. They can change easy. Four figures into five, five figures into six. They just need a little attention. Now people… we grow up, get older, our numbers go up—but we end. Everyone ends at zero, right back where we started. But numbers…if you play them right…they keep going up and up and up. Even after you're gone. The money lives on…it's all that's left of us when we go.

**CARLA.** How fascinating. I should get going.

**FRED.** Of course.

**CARLA.** Nice meeting you.

    *(CARLA goes, off. FRED looks around. TYLER looks at NINA.)*

**TYLER.** I give up. What's the question.

    *(Pause.)*

**NINA.** I came here because—so much time has passed. And I understand …at the time, maybe our passions got the best of us. We couldn't see clearly, we were too close to what was happening. But…a lot of time has passed now. So what I want to know is… Do you understand that what you did to me—was wrong?

**TYLER.** I said I'm sorry.

**NINA.** Right. But do you see that what you did was wrong?

**TYLER.** I'm sorry I caused you pain.

**NINA.** No…not that you caused me pain. That what you did to me was wrong.

**TYLER.** I don't understand the difference.

**NINA.** You don't.

**TYLER.** No.

**NINA.** Then…I think I'm gonna go.

**TYLER.** You know…you come here…you say so much time has passed. But you haven't changed a bit. When you're ready to join the real world, call me.

    *(TYLER rises.)*

**NINA.** I don't want the real world. I want a better world.

**TYLER.** Do you! Well, life doesn't work that way! This is it…it's what's in front of your face, not what you wish in your little girl dreams. Goodbye.

    *(TYLER goes, off. NINA looks down at her table. FRED turns to her.)*

**FRED.** I couldn't help overhearing you.

**NINA.** Oh…sorry about that.

**FRED.** No… Do you believe that?

**NINA.** What?

**FRED.** What you just said…that you don't want the real world. That you want a better world.

**NINA.** I do. Don't you. Doesn't everyone? Why else would you—get up in the morning? Why else would you agree to meet an ex-boyfriend in a restaurant? Or speak to a stranger? Why would you do those things if not…to make the world better? To make the world you want to live in?

**FRED.** Hmm. That's interesting. Thanks.

(*FRED turns back to his table.*)

**NINA.** I couldn't help overhearing you.

**FRED.** Oh?

**NINA.** Who—died?

**FRED.** Oh. A colleague. Cancer. Like that.

**NINA.** I'm sorry.

**FRED.** Which is—why I asked you that question, actually. Because…seeing him die. I thought…and I've been thinking ever since— This is it. Here you have it. The real world. As real as it gets. This moment, now. So what's the use in dreaming of a better world. What's the use being angry or dissatisfied with what you have. It can all leave you at any moment, all of it, so why not be happy with what's in front of you.

(*Short pause. NINA takes a step to* FRED.)

He called, right? The ex? Some people never hear from their ex's again. He said he was sorry. He admitted he caused you pain. Maybe he didn't say what you wished he would say…but it's something. This woman I was on the date with… I didn't like her much, I wasn't very attracted to her, she was obviously sort of shallow. But. She agreed to go on a date with me. There she was, sitting in front of me. Doing her best to live in a difficult world. Real. There. So why not look at her in that light…the light of what's real, instead of what I might wish for. Anyway…at the least, that's just what I've been thinking lately.

(*NINA looks off, where* TYLER *exited.*)

Are you going to go after him?

**NINA.** I…don't know.

(*She looks towards the exit. As she starts to go,* FRED *speaks, boldly.*)

**FRED.** Do you like strawberry bread pudding?

(*NINA turns to* FRED, *looks at him. A beat. He smiles. Slow fade to black.*)

### *End of Play*

# LIBERAL ARTS COLLEGE
## by Lucy Thurber

**Required royalties must be paid every time this play is performed before any audience, whether or not it is presented for profit and whether or not admission is charged.** Inquiries concerning rights, including stock and amateur performance rights, you must contact:

**Playscripts, Inc.**
website:   www.playscripts.com
email:     info@playscripts.com
phone:     1-866-NEW-PLAY (639-7529)

Inquiries concerning all other rights should be addressed to the author's agent: Beth Blickers, Abrams Artists Agency, 275 Seventh Avenue, 26th Floor, New York, NY 10001.

# BIOGRAPHY

Lucy Thurber is the author of seven plays: *Where We're Born, Ashville, Scarcity, Killers and Other Family, Stay, Bottom of The World* and *Monstrosity.* The Atlantic Theater Company opened its 2007/08 season with *Scarcity.* Rattlestick Playwrights Theater has produced three of her plays, *Where We're Born, Killers and Other Family,* and *Stay. Bottom of The World* was commissioned and workshopped by Women's Expressive Theater, Inc. at the Eugene O'Neill, the first Tribeca Theater Festival and The Public Theater. *Monstrosity* was workshopped at Encore Theatre Company (San Francisco). She was the recipient of the 2000-2001 Manhattan Theatre Club Playwriting Fellowship and has been a guest artist at Alaska's Perseverance Theatre twice, where she helped to adapt both *Desire Under The Elms* and *Moby Dick.* She has had readings and workshops at Manhattan Theatre Club, The New Group, Primary Stages, MCC Theater, Encore Theatre Company, PlayPenn, Williamstown Theatre Festival, New River Dramatists and Soho Rep. She was one of three playwrights in residence at The Orchard Project, summer 2007. Her 10-minute play *Dinner* is published in *Not So Sweet,* a collection of plays from Soho Rep's 10 minute play festival. *Scarcity* was published in the December 2007 issue of American Theatre. Her produced plays are published by Dramatists Play Service. Ms. Thurber is a member of New Dramatists, 13P, MCC Playwrights Coalition and Dorothy Strelsin New American Writers Group at Primary Stages. She is currently writing a new play under commission from Playwrights Horizons. She is the recipient of the 1st Gary Bonasorte Memorial Prize for Playwriting 2008. She has taught at Columbia University in Graduate Playwriting and currently teaches at Sarah Lawrence College. She also runs an after school playwriting program for New York City teenagers through MCC Theater.

# ACKNOWLEDGMENTS

*Liberal Arts College* was originally produced by The 24 Hour Company in association with At Play Productions at The Atlantic Theater on the set of *Parlour Song* in New York City on March 17, 2008. It featured the following cast:

| | |
|---|---|
| TESSA | Melissa Joyner |
| JAMIE | Jess Weixler |
| ELIZABETH | Zoe Anastassiou |
| HEIDI | Lauren Hines |

## CAST OF CHARACTERS

TESSA
JAMIE
ELIZABETH
HEIDI

## THE TONE

Sweet, funny, overly dramatic—between the beats it's simple/true and then the end is a return to normal. You know, liberal arts girls.

# LIBERAL ARTS COLLEGE

TESSA *and* JAMIE *asleep in bed.* ELIZABETH *stands above them and stares down.* ELIZABETH *begins to weep.* TESSA *and* JAMIE *continue to sleep.* ELIZABETH *weeps harder.* JAMIE *wakes up.*

**JAMIE.** What's wrong?

**ELIZABETH.** You weren't at your dorm.

**JAMIE.** What's wrong?

**ELIZABETH.** Just because I let a lot of people touch me doesn't mean they touch me.

**JAMIE.** Okay.

**ELIZABETH.** You allow yourself to be touched. Don't you?

**JAMIE.** I think so.

**TESSA.** *(Keeping her eyes closed:)* I am sleeping. I am fucken sleeping. Do the two of you care that I am sleeping?

*(*JAMIE *gets out of bed and moves to the table.* ELIZABETH *follows.)*

**ELIZABETH.** Do you think I'm a whore?

**JAMIE.** No.

**ELIZABETH.** I have an IQ of 181. Technically speaking my intellect is bigger than my emotions it makes me frigid. Not physically. Physically I'm very sensual. Physically I understand about fucking and I like to fuck.

**JAMIE.** Should I make some coffee? *(Calling:)* Hey Tessa do you want some coffee?

*(*TESSA *jumps out of bed and crosses to the table.)*

**TESSA.** *(To* JAMIE:*)* You are in my kitchen!

**JAMIE.** Obviously.

**TESSA.** What did I say to you a minute ago!?

**ELIZABETH.** Hi Tessa.

**TESSA.** Hi Elizabeth. What did I say to you Jamie?

**JAMIE.** Why are you yelling at me?

**TESSA.** You're kidding right? Every time you have too much to drink, you pass out here and practically push me off the bed all night and I have not been sleeping you know I haven't been sleeping and you know why?

**ELIZABETH.** Why?

**JAMIE.** She has insomnia.

**TESSA.** That is a secret. You know that's a secret—!

**JAMIE.** And I didn't pass out. You live off campus, the buses stop running, what do you want me to do? Walk home—?

**TESSA.** Campus shuttle Jamie! Campus shuttle. You know I have a problem saying no to people and you're never sensitive to that.

**JAMIE.** Jesus! Do we have to do this right now? Elizabeth is really going through something—

**TESSA.** Right. What about what I need?

(TESSA *storms back to the bed.*)

**ELIZABETH.** You should talk to her. I always cause problems. Why do I always cause problems?

**JAMIE.** I offered her coffee. I offered to make her coffee. Oh my God what a horrible thing to do?

(HEIDI *enters.*)

**HEIDI.** (*To* JAMIE:) Hi I was wondering if maybe you took my car?

**JAMIE.** No—

**ELIZABETH.** Hi Heidi.

**HEIDI.** Hi Elizabeth. (*To* JAMIE:) You didn't take my car?

**JAMIE.** No.

**HEIDI.** I think Mark took my car.

**ELIZABETH.** I hate that guy.

**HEIDI.** I know. I can't find my car. I think he took it. My Dad is going to be mad at me. He told me not to loan Mark my car. My Dad doesn't like Mark.

**ELIZABETH.** Nobody likes Mark.

**HEIDI.** He calls me little buddy. I don't like being called little buddy. It's not feminine.

**ELIZABETH.** You're very feminine.

**HEIDI.** Thank you. I have issues with that.

**JAMIE.** She shouldn't. You're very feminine.

(TESSA *crosses back.*)

**TESSA.** (*To* JAMIE:) I can't believe you! Hi Heidi.

**HEIDI.** Hi Tessa.

**TESSA.** (*To* JAMIE:) I can't believe you!

**JAMIE.** You just said that.

**HEIDI.** (*To* TESSA:) Mark stole my car. I broke up with him.

**TESSA.** Mark's an asshole. (*To* JAMIE:) I've been crying in the bedroom and you don't care.

**ELIZABETH.** Of course she cares. Don't you care Jamie?

**TESSA.** If you cared you would have come to comfort me. You are emotionally available to everybody but me. I told you I needed sleep. Why couldn't you respect that?

**HEIDI.** I wish he hadn't taken my car. I really like my car.

**ELIZABETH.** *(To* HEIDI*:)* I'm emotionally frigid and you're the opposite. You let anyone inside you.

**TESSA.** It's true Heidi. She's right. You've got really bad boundaries.

*(Beat.)*

**HEIDI.** I'm lonely. I feel funny because I'm lonely all the time.

**JAMIE.** *(To* HEIDI *and* ELIZABETH*:)* She comes from such a nice family. At Christmas they all get stockings. She has a brother and a sister. Her house has a front yard and a back yard. They have a dog.

**ELIZABETH.** Do you ever feel like you are a photocopy? Like just a Xerox?

**HEIDI.** I like Mark. I broke up with him, nobody likes him but I like him. I like his eyes and his mouth and the stupid way he drools on my shoulder when he sleeps.

**TESSA.** Sometimes when I look in the mirror I say, who am I? Who am I? Who am I? Who am I?

**JAMIE.** I played catch with her little brother. Her Dad bought me a stupid funny doll. And I thought this is my reward. For being so good and waiting so long this is my reward.

**ELIZABETH.** I can't feel my fingers sometimes. I move them when I talk. I think it makes me look smart, intricate hand movements moving along with intricate thoughts, but I can't feel them.

**HEIDI.** I'm home sick.

**ELIZABETH.** I'm home sick.

**TESSA.** Every day of my life has been the same, till I came here. I have four years and then everything will be the same again.

**JAMIE.** If I don't move, if I hold really still, I can slow this down so it will last forever. Four years are forever.

*(Beat.)*

**TESSA.** I wish Mark hadn't stolen your car. I really want pancakes.

**JAMIE.** Pancakes sound awesome!

**HEIDI.** I know! Fucken Mark. Brunch would be so perfect right now.

**ELIZABETH.** We could call a cab.

**JAMIE.** I don't have money for a cab.

**HEIDI.** Don't worry. We've got you.

**ELIZABETH.** Yeah. We've got you.

**TESSA.** *(Putting her arm around* JAMIE*:)* I've got money.

**JAMIE.** *(To* TESSA*:)* I'll call the cab. Will you grab out coats?

*(*TESSA *hands* JAMIE *her cell-phone and exits to get their coats.)*

**ELIZABETH.** I want to smoke. Heidi?

**HEIDI.** I'm quitting.

**ELIZABETH.** Today?

**HEIDI.** No. I'll quit tomorrow. *(They exit to smoke.)*

    *(JAMIE dials.)*

    *(Lights Down.)*

## *End of Play*

# K, X, Z AND V
## by Ian Williams

## BIOGRAPHY

Ian Williams pretended to speak for his generation in non-fiction and journalism for a few years before helping start a few dot-coms, writing Off Broadway plays, and generally dorking out in several bizarre areas. He has written for *The New York Times*, *The Washington Post*, *Salon*, and even produced some of the movie trailers you missed while in line for popcorn. His blog (xtcian.com) was featured in *The New York Times Magazine* in 2005 after he threatened to secede from the Union.

He now writes and develops television and movies with his wife Tessa. Along with daughter Lucy, they live in Los Angeles when they're not pollinating their pumpkins in upstate New York.

## ACKNOWLEDGMENTS

*K, X, Z and V* was originally produced by The 24 Hour Company at Bleecker Street Theater in New York City on August 6, 2000. It was directed by Jeremy Dobrish with the following cast:

| | |
|---|---|
| TRENT | Sean Wiliams |
| JAMES | Seth Shelden |
| MADELINE | Sarah Clarke |
| SHEILA | Amanda Quaid |
| BOSS | Joseph Balint |

## CAST OF CHARACTERS

TRENT
JAMES
MADELINE
SHEILA
BOSS

# K, X, Z AND V

*On the stage sits two tables; one completely empty, the other crammed with as much silly crap as possible—teddy bears, wigs, superman outfits, board games, flowers, etc.*

*After a few seconds, two men and two women walk in. They see the table full of items and stop short, as though they've seen this setup before. Horror creeps through them.*

**TRENT.** Oh no.

**JAMES.** Is this what I think it is?

**TRENT.** No fucking way. There is NO WAY we're going to be stuck doing this again.

**JAMES.** *(To one of the women:)* Madeline, did you know about this?

*(MADELINE is obviously the leader of this little troupe. They all sit at the empty table.)*

**MADELINE.** No, but let's not jump to conclusions. Until he actually SAYS it, then we don't know that's why we're here.

**TRENT.** Why the hell else would we be here in this room full of shit? You KNOW he's going to stick it to us again.

**JAMES.** Remember last time?

**MADELINE.** We are paid to do whatever he wants us to do. If he wants us to come in here and do *handsprings* for an hour, then that's what we're going to do.

**TRENT.** *(Bleary-eyed:)* I should have gone to grad school. I should have stayed in Prague. I always wanted to learn oboe…

**JAMES.** Did he want to meet us *here*, like in this room?

**MADELINE.** Yes. And he said it was excruciatingly important.

**TRENT.** *(To nobody in particular:)* It's not too late. I could always run out the fire escape…

**MADELINE.** I think he…

*(SHEILA, the other girl, has already raised her hand.)*

Yes, Sheila?

**SHEILA.** *(Unbelievably shy:)* I…I can't do a handspring.

*(General clamor by all involved. Before MADELINE can respond, a dour, older BOSS walks in wearing a suit. They all stop and look straight at him. He holds a small orange vial of pills aloft.)*

*(Deliberately, he places the vial of pills in the middle of the empty table, where they all stare at it. He speaks with an unamused drawl.)*

203

**BOSS.** This…is your charge. You are to name this drug. You are to give it a name worthy of the company we all call home. I have been through focus group after focus group, and every name they have come up with…SUCKS.

*(The* BOSS *motions to the table full of props and baubles.)*

*(With gruff disdain:)* Here's your table full of creative…crap…whatever. Use it to open up your channels or some shit like that…This drug needs a name, and you've got to give it one. You're the last stop, folks.

**MADELINE.** When do you need it, sir?

**BOSS.** Fifteen minutes.

*(They are stunned.)*

**MADELINE.** …Fifteen minutes?

**TRENT.** Um, sir, the last time we had this project, it took three weeks—

**BOSS.** I'm aware of that. People, we have a press conference at exactly TWO in the P.M. this afternoon, and if this drug doesn't have a name, we can't talk about it. And the shareholders will react accordingly, and then some somebodies around here will be out of a job. You got it?

**MADELINE.** Yes sir.

**BOSS.** *(Plops a spec sheet in front of* MADELINE:*)* Hit a home run for me, people.

*(He exits. They wait for the door to slam offstage.)*

**TRENT.** I TOLD you! I fucking TOLD you!

**JAMES.** Fifteen minutes?

**MADELINE.** Now let's not freak out here. This can be done. We just need to concentrate.

**TRENT.** They spend 25 million dollars on agencies to come up with these drug names and they always come back to us!

**JAMES.** This isn't our department, Madeline. We're only supposed to be doing the directions and packaging copy.

**MADELINE.** *(Scans the spec sheet.)* Look, let's just see what the drug does and take it from there.

**JAMES.** What is the drug's real name?

**TRENT.** *(With utter sarcasm:)* I dunno, maybe "Terrance"? "Bjorn"? Why do you care what the drug's real name is James?

**JAMES.** Because, dickhead, sometimes you can get a good idea from the real name, just shorten it or something.

**MADELINE.** *(Reads:)* Phenzo-disporine-cyclio-toro-ketorolac.

*(Another stunned silence.)*

**JAMES.** Yeah, maybe "Bjorn" IS a good idea.

**TRENT.** *(Points at other table:)* But THIS is the most insulting thing. The corporate idea of creativity. Lock you in a fluorescent room with a bunch of really wacky WIGS and TEDDY BEARS.

**MADELINE.** Look, they're just trying to help us out. If we go through this thing step by step, we'll generate a name in no time.

**TRENT.** I don't "generate." I "write."

**MADELINE.** *(Reads:)* It "assist in post-adolescent continence regularity during circadian cycles."

> *(They all stop for a second. SHEILA summons the bravery to speak in a crackly voice.)*

**SHEILA.** Adult bed-wetting.

**TRENT.** *(After a beat:)* It's a drug for adult bed-wetting?

**MADELINE.** Look like it, yes.

**JAMES.** Wow. This one's going to be tough.

**TRENT.** God. "PeeNoMore"? "UrineBeGone"?

**MADELINE.** We're going to stick to the rules.

**JAMES.** *All* the rules?

**MADELINE.** Let us reiterate them so that they are fresh in our heads. Number one. The drug must sound like the future. We want our users to have a cure straight from the 21st century. So what does that mean?

**JAMES, TRENT, and SHEILA.** *(By rote, with TRENT being especially bored:)* K, X, Z and V.

**MADELINE.** All drugs must have a K, X, Z or V in the title.

**TRENT.** You know, those are all really valuable Scrabble tiles as well.

**JAMES.** You can't use proper names in Scrabble.

**MADELINE.** Think Vicodin, Valium, Xanax, Zolotrin.

**TRENT.** What about Morphine? That's a great drug name without those letters.

**MADELINE.** *(Speaks like she's said this many times before:)* Which brings me to rule number two. The drug must sound like what it treats—while also conjuring subconscious images of comfort.

**JAMES.** *(Scribbling:)* Morphine—like Morpheus, the god of dreams.

**TRENT.** Prozac?

> *(Sensing the challenge, MADELINE puts the paper down.)*

**MADELINE.** It is "pro," meaning "forward"—along with the 21st century "Z."

**TRENT.** Zoloft.

**MADELINE.** Brings the user to a "loftier" place.

**TRENT.** Paxil.

**JAMES.** Pax means "peace" in Latin.

**MADELINE.** Brings peace of mind to users.

**TRENT.** Ritalin and Adderol.

**MADELINE.** Takes out riddled and addled kids and makes them calm again.

**TRENT.** Jesus, does the American public know they're being drugged by the NAMES of drugs too?

**MADELINE.** It's not ours to question.

**TRENT.** Madeline, I don't get how you can be such an automaton about it. I mean, they give us this table full of arty shit and yet you want us to name this drug the same old thing?

**MADELINE.** I know what works and we're sticking with it.

**TRENT.** You know, you amaze me. Women are the ones that are supposed to be most in touch with the irrational, magical side of things, and every woman in this company—no offense, Sheila—is a freakin' ROBOT.

**MADELINE.** That's because we have to work twice as hard to get half the respect that you—

**TRENT.** Oh please, don't even trot THAT one out. This isn't 1975. You make TWICE what I make.

**MADELINE.** I'm also responsible for everything this team does.

**TRENT.** We got stuck in this same room six months ago on that stomach acid-reducing drug. Three weeks, and you made us go with AXID.

**MADELINE.** That's because it "X's" the "ACID" in you.

> *(All three of them besides* TRENT *make an X with their forearms, then point at "you" in unison with her sentence.)*

**TRENT.** God, here I am on Planet ZYMOXX. What is wrong with you people?

**MADELINE.** We are trying to get this drug named and you're not helping!

> *(*TRENT *is in her face now.)*

**TRENT.** Okay: Zaxxon! Zirconia! Valvoklex! Xaxamonium! Zizaxaxavaizixaxazaa!

**MADELINE.** Sit down, you bastard!

**JAMES.** Honey, don't let him upset you.

> *(The action stops;* JAMES *knows he screwed up.)*

**TRENT.** What did you just call her?

**JAMES.** Nothing.

**TRENT.** You called her…you called her…

**SHEILA.** *(Quietly:)* Honey…

**TRENT.** Yeah, that. Are you two DATING?

**MADELINE.** It's none of your business.

**TRENT.** James has been my best friend since high school. It damn well IS my business.

**JAMES.** About three weeks. Dude, I was going to tell you—

**TRENT.** Three weeks?

**MADELINE.** The fact is, Trent, you've become totally insufferable. James won't say it, but I will. Your rampant negativity had made working with you unbearable, and it has made James avoid you.

**JAMES.** Now, Maddie, come on—

**TRENT.** "Maddie?"

**MADELINE.** *(With hatred:)* Something is wrong deep inside of you, Trent. Half the time I've wished I could shovel a few of these drugs into YOU.

**TRENT.** What, just because I'm the only person here that still wants to have a PERSONALITY?

**MADELINE.** You don't have a personality, you just want to make everyone uncomfortable!

**TRENT.** Some of us don't NEED a "creative table" to get ideas, you android. *(Points to other table.)* My brain ALREADY LOOKS LIKE THAT!

**MADELINE.** Then why don't you USE it for something USEFUL?

**TRENT.** I've got a drug for you, Madeline! It's a suppository called Zerxovicozax and you can SHOVE IT UP YOUR ASS!

**JAMES.** Trent, God damnit, don't talk to her like that!

**TRENT.** What the fuck do YOU have to say about it—

> *(With this, all three start a loud, awful argument for several seconds until:)*

**SHEILA.** *(Yells:)* CHUCHOTEZ! *[Pronounced shoo-show-tay.]*

> *(They stop in stunned silence.)*

**MADELINE.** What?

**SHEILA.** *(In regular voice:)* Chuchotez. *(Spells it out in the air with her fingers.)* Chuchotez. It's French for "whisper."

> *(The others still stand as SHEILA continues, amazed that she is talking. SHEILA takes out one single pill and places it on the table. She speaks with a deliberate, unaffected innocence.)*

I think about the boy in grade school, you know, the one who gets hit by the dodgeball and doesn't have any friends? He can't go to sleepovers because he always has an accident in the bed. Maybe his schoolmates find out and they tease him abut it clear until he gets to college.

> *(TRENT seems singularly mesmerized by her dialogue.)*

Then he's an adult, in the working world, but still the problem won't go away. He feels cursed by God. He can never love a woman, can never tell anyone his problem. *(Holds up pill.)* But then this little white thing comes along, and it is his salvation. He cries out for help, and this little white pebble says "chuchotez."

> *(A beat, then:)*

**MADELINE.** Chuchotez.

**JAMES.** It's got a Z in it.

**MADELINE.** The Z is silent.

**JAMES.** It sounds like what it does.

**MADELINE.** We could make it "chuchoTAB."

**JAMES.** That's good.

**MADELINE.** It's excellent. Chuchotab 50 mg. We've done it. *(Excited:)* Let's go tell him.

> *(JAMES and MADELINE exit. TRENT speaks in his regular, loud tenor but the words are twisted somehow.)*

**TRENT.** Can you believe what they're doing? Can you believe that—

> *(Before he finishes, she gives him a sweet, long kiss. She draws back, his eyes left open wide. He tries to speak again.)*

Just to…be so… I think they—

> *(SHEILA presses one finger to his lips, then smiles.)*

**SHEILA.** Whisper.

> *(Blackout.)*

## End of Play

# BE STILL
## by Stephen Winter

## BIOGRAPHY

Stephen Winter wrote and directed the film *Chocolate Babies*. He also produced the film *Tarnation* by Jonathan Caouette.

## ACKNOWLEDGMENTS

*Be Still* was originally produced by The 24 Hour Company at Bleecker Street Theatre in New York City on February 25, 2001. It was directed by Angel David with the following cast:

RENE ....................................................................... Rene Alberta
JOSEPH ................................................................. Joe Lattimore
EMILY................................................................. Emily Conbere
DONNA......................................................... Donna DuPlantier

## CAST OF CHARACTERS

RENE, a beautiful, tough, dynamic Americanized Island woman who is near 60. She has a slight accent and a loud voice. It doesn't have to be a specific Caribbean accent. She wears a very smart dark suit with sharp jewelry and maybe has a streak of grey in her hair. She has a foul mouth but is NOT coarse. She is elegant and passionate.

JOSEPH, a ghost. In life he was an Island man and a cad.

EMILY, an Island woman. Funny, dizzy yet surprisingly tenacious. She speaks with a strange, lilting turn of phrase.

DONNA, Rene's best friend. American, 20 years younger and more trendy in style. She is sassy, arty, and slightly in awe of Rene and her strength of character.

## NOTES

This play should be light on the props. An easy chair will be needed for the end. VOICES are needed backstage to sing a "Jesus" song.

# BE STILL

*Dark stage, stark spotlight, RENE firmly enters and stops at the front of the stage.*

**RENE.** Me no care for NONE of you mothafuckers, this Negro is going in the ground TODAY!!

*(Lights go half up. This is Rene's apartment. JOSEPH enters wearing a dark suit. He is always slowly stalking around the edges of the scene.)*

**JOSEPH.** She got the call from Canada. When Canada calls it's bad news.

**RENE.** When the Island cousins can't get through to my cell phone or remember the damn number or whatever, they call the Canada cousins and Canada calls me when it's bad news like this.

**JOSEPH.** Every other day for the rest of your life.

**RENE.** And I had a GOOD listing! With good white folks and I lost it because I had to fly to the Island for HIM! See, I get tired of dealing with these Negroes cause they take up all of your time looking at property but then they don't have the cash or their credit don't check out for the woman talk them out of it, it's always some shit!

**JOSEPH.** When do you want to see me again?

**RENE.** But white folks are EASY to work with! They don't waste no time! They don't want you in their neighborhood so they give you what you want and let you leave! *(Pause.)* I used to resent that shit, now I love it!

**JOSEPH.** Every other day for the rest of your life.

*(Lights on "The Island" are very bright. Dressed in bright colors, EMILY rushes in carrying a clipboard and a list.)*

**EMILY.** Oh Missy Gathers! Missy Gathers! Such an unhappy day!

**RENE.** How much?

**EMILY.** Misser Gathers was such a good Christian man.

**RENE.** He certainly thought so. How much?

**EMILY.** Please to accept my every condolence.

**RENE.** Thank you dear. How much?

**EMILY.** I want to make you as comfortable as possible.

**RENE.** Ma'am, don't worry bout me!

**EMILY.** Everything on the list come to 40,000.

**RENE.** American?

**EMILY.** No! No! Island exchange.

**RENE.** But 40,000! What are you dressing him in, gold?

**EMILY.** *(Proudly:)* Only the BEST for Misser Gathers! We have the lovely wine cherry oak coffin, brass handles, raw silk and of course, guaranteed waterproofing!

**RENE.** What a comfort...

**EMILY.** *(Reads list:)* For full service, pastor fees, chapel rental, body preparations, flower procurement, the procurement of the stone, the engraving of the stone, the digging of the hole, the covering of the hole...25,000.

**RENE.** Damn...

**EMILY.** *(Continues list:)* The exhuming of the body, the preparation of the body, the cremation of the body—

**RENE.** What?!? What? The what?

**EMILY.** Cremation is 15,000.

**RENE.** Why are you cremating the body you buried?

**EMILY.** It says this to do so here on my list.

**RENE.** I said cremate him the day I hear he died! Then I called back and said bury him instead! Why would I bury the man, dig his ass up just to burn him?

**EMILY.** Misser Gathers would want cremation! He would want his dust to be spread across the beautiful island that he love so!

**RENE.** Misser Gathers spread enough love in his time. I ain't paying to spread him a moment more!

**EMILY.** Misser Gathers left money to do what's right!

**RENE.** Misser Gathers spent his savings on bitches and booze! He died a pauper! Missy Gathers is paying!

**EMILY.** *(Pause.)* No cremation now?

**RENE.** No.

**EMILY.** Cremation finish?

**RENE.** Yes! Damn! *(Walks away.)* Joseph, Joseph! Pain to the END!

**JOSEPH.** It's a relief when your yard girl Donna finally arrives. You've been friends for years and she ALWAYS knows the right thing to say.

*(DONNA strides towards RENE. JOSEPH exits quietly.)*

**DONNA.** Honey, if you don't calm down and take a breath you gonna end up dressing, acting, gaspin' and heaving exactly like Sandy Dennis in "Come Back To The Five And Dime Jimmy Dean, Jimmy Dean" and that would be too bad too bad!

**RENE.** Shut up, Donna! These Negroes think I'm full of guilt and sorrow and ready to pay for anything.

**DONNA.** Guess they now know you ain't exactly distraught. *(Looks around.)* Lovely day for a service. Look at all these old women CRY!

**RENE.** They love Joseph here. And he loved them.

**DONNA.** Weepin' n' wailin' n' gnashing they teeth!

**RENE.** Those heifers starts rending garments I'm gonna need a drink!

**DONNA.** Well, you know a nigga's funeral ain't over till one of this bitches pitch herself in the coffin. But it ain't gonna be me.

**RENE.** And it ain't gonna be me. *(Pause, low gospel singing is heard offstage.)* Damn!

**DONNA.** *(Starts to clap.)* Well c'mon now. No need showin' all your cousins what a heathen you became.

**RENE.** I don't know the words!

**DONNA.** Just follow me. "Jeeeeezuz! Jeeeeezuz! Jeeeeezuz! Jeezuz! Jeezuz!" SING woman!

**RENE and DONNA.** "Jeeeeezuz! Jeeeeezuz! Jeeeeezuz! Jeezuz! Jeezuz!"

*(They sing and bounce till the song finishes. RENE sighs. Then singing starts up again offstage, same song only this time faster. RENE throws up her hands.)*

**RENE.** I need a drink.

**DONNA.** Later…

**RENE.** I need a joint!

**DONNA.** Later! Try to think something good about the man. Try to remember a good time.

*(JOSEPH enters dressed in a t-shirt. He grabs RENE and brings her to the front of the stage. RENE is now 18. They kiss passionately. JOSEPH is macking hard.)*

**JOSEPH.** It's like I feel you going all through me.

**RENE.** Oh, me too…me too.

**JOSEPH.** Me too what?

**RENE.** I feel you…too.

**JOSEPH.** You are so beautiful.

**RENE.** Oh Joseph…

**JOSEPH.** But baby, can you take me? 'Cause I'm a big guy, you understand.

**RENE.** Yes…

**JOSEPH.** There's a lot of me and a lot of women want this. It takes a strong lady to handle it. You understand? If you want me… You listening?

**RENE.** My mother is waiting up.

**JOSEPH.** I know… *(Leans in.)* There's a lot of me to take. Do you want this?

**RENE.** My father is waiting for me too.

**JOSEPH.** Oh… *(Backs off.)* Well…um…

**RENE.** *(Suddenly:)* I want it! *(Pause, smile.)* I do. So…when do you want to see me again?

**JOSEPH.** *(Approaches, smiles.)* Every other day for the rest of your life?

    *(They kiss again.* JOSEPH *slips offstage and* RENE *returns to present.)*

**DONNA.** That's sweet.

**RENE.** That's Negro bullshit! "Every other day for the rest of m—" and what happens in the meantimes? Claudia! Rhonda! Sara! Sandra!

**DONNA.** That kiss sounds sweet.

**RENE.** That kiss was. Almost forty years…and I can still…taste…

    *(*EMILY *bounds in, now dressed in mourning clothes.)*

**EMILY.** Oh, Missy Gathers, Missy Gathers. Such a sad, sad day for Missy Gathers.

**RENE.** It was a beautiful service dear.

**DONNA.** We LOVED the singing.

**EMILY.** Missy Gathers, Gravedigger finish. We no have no hole.

**RENE.** You what?

**EMILY.** Gravedigger finish. No hole for Misser Gathers.

**RENE.** Gravedigger WHAT?

**DONNA.** You BASTARD!!!!!!

**EMILY.** Gravedigger back Tuesday, we finish Misser Gathers then for sure.

**RENE.** I'm not coming back Tuesday! I'm not staying another MOMENT! See those boys, those cousins over there! Give them a shovel! They'll dig a damn hole! In fact, take my earrings, take my shoes! I'LL dig the damn hole MYSELF!

**EMILY.** But Missy Gathers!

**RENE.** *(Shouts:)* Me no care for NONE of you mothafuckers, this Negro is going in the ground TODAY!!

    *(Lights go down low with* RENE *spotlighted.* EMILY *and* DONNA *freeze.* RENE *turns to audience.)*

**RENE.** Needless to say…she found me a hole.

    *(Either* EMILY *and* DONNA *bring a chair onstage then leave.* RENE *is back home and starts taking off her jacket, earrings, shoes and chuckles and mutters to herself. Slowly* JOSEPH *returns wearing his suit.)*

**RENE.** Every other day for the rest of my life…

**JOSEPH.** You took everything I had inside, everything I could give. You took until I hurt. I feel you going all through me. Always.

**RENE.** *(Laughing:)* Gravedigger finish! Oh Missy Gathers, Missy Gathers…

**JOSEPH.** I learned I didn't have that much in me. You always had more. I still feel that too.

**RENE.** Back in my condo. Back home. It's cold here.

**JOSEPH.** It was warm on the Island.

**RENE.** Every other day…

**JOSEPH.** …for the rest of your life.

**RENE.** I bought this place cause it's high up. Twenty fourth floor. No one can see me from the street.

**JOSEPH.** Oh, baby…

*(Lights start to slowly go down.)*

**RENE.** The lady who lived here before— This Jewish lady…

**JOSEPH.** She dead.

**RENE.** She died right in here. Ninety-tree years old.

**JOSEPH.** You are so beautiful.

**RENE.** But I kept her name on the door so no one lookin' for me knows I'm in here.

**JOSEPH.** "Missus Rachel Drubowski."

**RENE.** *(Sits in chair.)* That's me!

**JOSEPH.** Oh baby…

**RENE.** Joseph's lookin' for me. I buried him on the Island but still… I get this feeling.

**JOSEPH.** *(Softly:)* My baby…

**RENE.** So when I walk in the house I always say real loud, "I'm here to do the house work Missus Drubowski!" *(Laughs.)* Joseph was slick but easily confused. He hasn't found me yet! DAMN!

**JOSEPH.** *(Whisper:)* When do you want to see me again?

**RENE.** Damn… *(Long pause, it's almost dark.)* Where are you Joe?

## End of Play

# Interested in producing your own event?

Please note that a licensing fee must be paid whenever The 24 Hour Plays event is produced, whether or not it is presented for profit, and whether or not admission is charged.

The 24 Hour Plays offers a production handbook to help you through the process. Please contact:

The 24 Hour Company
www.24hourplays.com
tina@24hourplays.com